MUHAMMAD ALI:
A MEMOIR

MUHAMMAD ALI: A MEMOIR

MICHAEL PARKINSON

HODDER &
STOUGHTON

First published in Great Britain in 2016 by Hodder & Stoughton
An Hachette UK company

2

A CIP catalogue record for this title is available from the British Library

Hardback ISBN: 978 1 473 65147 0
Trade Paperback ISBN: 978 1 473 65148 7
Ebook ISBN: 978 1 473 65149 4

Typeset by Palimpsest Book Production Ltd, Falkirk, Stirlingshire
Printed and bound by Clays Ltd, St Ives plc

Hodder & Stoughton policy is to use papers that are natural, renewable and
recyclable products and made from wood grown in sustainable forests.
The logging and manufacturing processes are expected to conform to the
environmental regulations of the country of origin.

Hodder & Stoughton Ltd
Carmelite House
50 Victoria Embankment
London EC4Y 0DZ

www.hodder.co.uk

CONTENTS

Me and my old sparring partner. I interviewed him four times and lost every one.

FOREWORD

LONGEVITY in the career that I have chosen means that whenever someone of cultural significance dies, you are one of the first ports of call for the alphabet soup of newsgathering in search of, for want of a better word, the Obituary interview. So, it was no great surprise that, in the days that followed the death of Muhammad Ali on 3 June 2016, I was asked to contribute my thoughts on the loss of this extraordinary man. The requests came from far and wide. From the United States to Sweden, India to Australia. Again, no surprise. You're not just talking about one of the greatest fighters of all time, but also one of the most significant social and cultural figures of the last century. The surprise was that as I answered more and more questions about Muhammad, it became increasingly

MUHAMMAD ALI: A MEMOIR

clear to me that – despite interviewing him four times between 1971 and 1981 – I had barely scratched the surface of this multifaceted personality.

At the end of the media interrogation, I felt I had not truly paid sufficient tribute to this man, and that he deserved better. This book is an attempt to do just that. In the following pages I try to understand and put into perspective the man, opposite whom I sat on four separate occasions, who thrilled, infuriated and bewildered me, but who never let me close enough to see what really made him tick, or explain the forces that shaped him.

I have been helped in my endeavour by my son Michael, who has contributed the historical spine of the book. Any inaccuracies, blame him. We have both been helped and are greatly indebted to the books on Ali written by Thomas Hauser, David Remnick, Ferdie Pacheco and to a lesser extent Norman Mailer, as well as the myriad articles and observations made about Ali throughout his life by friends, contemporaries, opponents and journalists. As someone who has spent a lifetime watching and reporting on sporting events and trying, at the same time, to compre-hend what separates the merely accomplished athlete from the great performer, I can think of no one else who attracted so many shrewd and accomplished observers to the task of explaining his virtuosity, both as a fighter and as a member of the human race.

My heartfelt thanks to Teresa Rudge, my long-suffering PA, for deciphering my handwriting and typing at the speed of light, and to my publisher and friend Roddy Bloomfield at Hodder and Stoughton, who immediately saw the worth of the project and nursed it to life.

Michael Parkinson
October 2016

PROLOGUE

IT wasn't love at first sight. To begin with I've always had an ambivalent attitude to boxing. As a kid I was a runner not a fighter. My father's attempts to give me a boxing lesson ended with my nose pouring blood and Dad spending a night in the spare room after a row with my manager who happened to be his wife. Then he took me to a boxing booth where we saw a young, slim, black boy poleaxe a challenger twice his size. When the victim later moved through the spectators, cap in hand begging coins, he had a lump the size of a large egg on his forehead. The victor was called Randolph Turpin, who many years later beat one of the greatest fighters of them all, Sugar Ray Robinson, had a brief spell as world champion, before losing the rematch and coming to a wretched end. As a young reporter I went to interview him. He was reading a kid's comic and didn't have much to say. Later he put a gun in his mouth and pulled the trigger.

Then, when I began writing about sport, I became friendly with Henry Cooper. We were booked together to appear at an event in Monaco where a blue-chip company was holding a conference. When we arrived at Heathrow for the outward journey, Henry discovered he had left his passport at home. Our Customs said they would let Henry out of the country but couldn't be certain of the reception in France, but they promised to contact the French authorities to warn them of the problem. Henry, a natural worrier, had nattered himself into a nervous wreck when we arrived. We were greeted by a French official who both looked and sounded like Inspector Clouseau. Henry tried to explain his problem with the missing passport. 'But my problem, Mr Cooper, is I don't know who you are,' Clouseau said. There followed a few minutes of argument, and I could see Henry, the mildest of men, becoming increasingly agitated. It was when Clouseau spread his arms, shrugged, and said, 'But you say you are a prizefighter, Mr Cooper. How do I know you are telling the truth?' Whereupon Henry lost it. Raising his left arm and pointing to ''enry's 'ammer' he said, 'If I hit you with this, mate, you'd know who I was.'

Clouseau started laughing. It had been a set-up.

The next time I saw 'Henry's Hammer' it was for real. It put Cassius Clay on his bum at Wembley in 1963, which led to the notorious 'torn glove' delay and the 'what if' that has intrigued British boxing fans every since. Clay caused terrible damage to Cooper's face, as did Muhammad Ali three years later. On both occasions Henry looked as though he had been hit by a wrecking ball. The second fight at Highbury was particularly gruesome, with blood spurting like a geyser from Cooper's eyebrow and the fighter's face a bloody mash. When we talked about it later Henry said, 'It didn't do much for my good looks. Ruined my modelling career.' When I asked him what it was like fighting Ali he replied, 'Like being in the ring with a bleeding tank.'

The boxer who descended the stairs on *Parkinson* in 1971 was beautiful. I could think of no description more appropriate. And I was not alone. An American sports-writer once said he would love to borrow Ali's physique for forty-eight hours because 'there are three guys I'd like to beat up and four women I want to make love to'. I was not to know that this would be the first of a series of interviews I would have with the boxer, which would last from the 1970s to the 1980s, and cover both the wondrous glory and the fearful downfall of the most singular human being I ever encountered.

He was a multitude of men, so whenever people ask me what he was like, I always ask them which Ali they want to talk about – the humorist, the radical activist, the man who fantasised he could fight every man in the whole wide world and beat the lot of them, or the childlike being who loved performing magic tricks and telling ghost stories. He was a one-man carnival quite unlike any other I ever encountered.

I was asked to present him with his award for Sportsman of the Millennium in 2000, but felt unable to encounter at close quarters that once glorious man who was now wrecked by a terrible illness. I had seen him on television being paraded in public, his face immobile and frozen, his eyes dull and lifeless, his voice, once a versatile instrument, now sounding like dry leaves rustled by an autumn wind. I remembered that beautiful man I had first encountered, dancing down the stairs to meet me, the humour, delivered with the skill of a great comedian, and the way in which – even when displaying the most aggressive and thunderous anger – he couldn't hide the playful glint in his eyes. Me: 'You are a public figure.' Ali: 'Did you call me a public nigger?'

I wanted to remember him as he once was and as he described himself: 'When will they ever have another fighter who writes poems, predicts rounds, beats everybody, makes people laugh, makes people cry, and is as tall and extra pretty as me? In the history of the world and from the beginning of time, there has never been another fighter like me.'

For once in his life you could accuse Muhammad Ali of being unduly modest.

Chapter 1

THE ROAD TO THE FIRST PARKINSON INTERVIEW

1942–1971

Ready to take on the world.

Chapter 1

'Ali evolved from a feared warrior to a benevolent monarch and ultimately to a benign venerated figure . . . who evokes feelings of respect and love.'

Thomas Hauser, *Muhammad Ali*

I F you assess Muhammad Ali purely as a boxer, he was a game-changer. Inside the ring, no one before or after looked or fought like him. He had the power and build of a heavyweight, with the grace and hand speed of Sugar Ray Robinson; the ring craft of a chess grandmaster with a fine line in psyching out his opponents, and he was blessed, if that is the correct word, with a chin made of granite and the heart of a lion – sadly, occasionally a particularly fool-hardy one. The veteran boxing commentator and analyst, Larry Merchant, once said: 'Ali was a warrior. He was in a hurting business, a hard business; the toughest game there is. And no matter what his style, underneath it all he was a tough son of a bitch . . . in the ring he was as tough a son of a bitch as anyone who ever lived.'

Outside the ring he was the supreme pugilist/ promoter, with the chutzpah of P. T. Barnum. He saw boxing as a branch of entertainment, and gave it mass-market appeal to both man and woman. Modern-day boxers with their untold riches should bend their knee to the man who took this brutal spectacle out of smoke-filled, backstreet halls and away from Mob control, changing how it was promoted, covered by the press and televised.

He was the most charismatic and dramatic boxer who ever crossed the ropes. He cast himself as a modern-day dragon slayer, tilting at the biggest windmills against impossible odds, with Angelo Dundee as his Sancho Panza and us, his adoring public, asked only to cheer from the sidelines whilst he howled at the moon. 'Ali, *bombaye!*' as the Zairians chanted on that fateful night in the jungle: 'Ali, kill him!'

As a result he became not just the biggest sports star, but the biggest star in the world, recognised and mobbed in both the shanty towns of Zaire and at Lenin's Tomb in Red Square. In his own words, with the gloves on, he 'shook up the world'. Perhaps the best boxer that ever drew breath. But that's not half the story.

*

'I'm not just a boxer, I'm taught by Elijah Muhammad, I'm educated. Even Oxford University, your biggest seat of learning, offered me a Professorship in Philosophy and Poetry to come in and teach. I'm not just an ordinary fighter, I can talk all week on millions of subjects and you do not have enough wisdom to corner me on television.'

Muhammad Ali on *Parkinson*, 1974

Ali was born into a segregated America, where legally, socially, educationally and economically black Americans were second-class citizens. In some areas of the South, where Ali grew up, they were viewed as subhuman. He was, from an early age, acutely aware of his standing being determined purely by the colour of his skin, and he questioned the basic fairness of this. When he turned professional, his strong sense of pride in his own race meant he refused to play the role of the 'Good Negro' that America demanded of its heavyweight champions. The revered Brown Bomber Joe Louis declared, 'The heavyweight champion should be the champion of all people.' Ali disagreed. He was only the champion of and for *his* people. His success and subsequent fame was a platform for him to teach in words and deeds that they deserved and could have a better deal in the world. 'I had to prove you could be a new kind of black man. I had to show that to the world.'

He was helped by the fact that his looks, physique and boxing prowess put the lie to the notion of white supremacy, and his lightning wit and charisma made him the darling of the press corps, ensuring that his name and message spread like wildfire through both the ghettoes of the black underclass and the drawing rooms of the white masters. Ali sought answers to the basic unfairness of his condition in the controversial teachings of Elijah Muhammad and his Nation of Islam. Before the Louisville Lip became its most devout of followers, this was a controversial movement masquerading as a religious sect. When Ali beat Liston for the second time, he had become the most high-profile spokesman for the Nation of Islam, placing the movement at the centre of the civil rights movement. Ali had become a self-styled Prophet of Allah in a Holy War against the white oppressors of the black men and women of America, and at the time he was hated and revered in equal measure. But Ali's beliefs were sincere and unshakeable. He was fearless in the ring, principled outside it. When he refused to join the US Army and was given a prison sentence, he was offered a deal. Join up and we'll give you a cushy job – personal appearances, exhibition boxing. Scornfully he turned the offer down because he understood the difference between a principle and a compromise, a legitimate deal and a backhander, even if it meant having the prime years of his boxing career taken from him.

Like most things he did in his life, Ali had called it right, and his return to boxing after his ban coincided with more enlightened, anti-authoritarian times, and the descent of Vietnam into a hellish and pointless stalemate. It was time for Ali to take back his title and mantle of 'the greatest', and for all Americans, black and white, to fall back in love with him, and follow him on the roller-coaster of his later career, marvelling and wincing at his three encounters with Joe Frazier and his victory against all odds in the steamy heat of Zaire against the formidable George Foreman.

Ali finally retired in 1981, years after he should have hung up his gloves, his health irreparably damaged by his inability to believe he was mortal. He spent the rest of his life in a kind of twilight world as the illness gradually robbed him of his voice, his grace, and ultimately his dignity.

*

By the time Ali died in 2016 he, like Mandela, had become a totemic figure, an American myth, a Once and Future King for the black people of America. The process began while he was alive, when in 1977 Marvel Comics teamed him up with Superman to take on alien invaders while his Nation of Islam brethren backed an 'autobiography' of Ali called *The Greatest* as long as they approved the content. During this period his image rights were sold for $50 million and the process of airbrushing and sanitising his life was completed. Consequently, by the time of Ali's death, he had become, in Thomas Hauser's opinion, a black Paul Bunyan, replete with legendary tales of derring-do that quickly became accepted wisdom. Everyone remembers when Ali threw his Olympic gold medal into the river because he was so incensed at being refused service in a Louisville diner. Well, actually he didn't, and neither did he reply to the waitress in said diner that 'I don't eat them neither' when she told him, 'We don't serve Negroes here.' But these and other stories have been co-opted, created and exaggerated by Ali and others to keep him alive and relevant for generations to come. And in his lifetime Ali did nothing to deny them. Nor did he lose his delight in telling them.

Myths are ciphers through which a people try to understand their past. They are, obviously, not a reliable way of understanding the true nature of a man who actually lived. Seen through the prism of this mythic status, Ali becomes untouchable and unreachable. Over time his rough edges are smoothed away, his life story airbrushed; his reputation becomes sacrosanct, inaccuracies that maintain this image become the truth. A sober assessment of a once-in-a-generation man is sacrificed on the altar of hagiography. For a man as thrilling, as challenging and as complex as Ali, this does him a disservice.

The problem is that, even when you strip away this protective layer, it is still difficult to find the real Ali. The renowned American sports journalist Ring Lardner once described his boxing style as a pebble skittering across the surface of a pond. The same could be said of any attempt to assess the man behind the myth. He was possessed of a personality like a kaleidoscope that changed with every twist. He was full of conflicts and contradictions.

He could be at one and the same time passionate, peevish, principled, pejorative, puritanical, predatory, a philanderer – but always a charmer and ever so pretty!

But let's start at the beginning and, as ever with Ali, the truth is more interesting than the authorised version.

Ali was born Cassius Marcellus Clay at Louisville General Hospital at 6.35 p.m. on 17 January 1942. His upbringing was black middle class. Unlike many of his later opponents, whom he would try to 'out-black', he was not from what was known as the black underclass. His father was a sign painter and occasional artist, and his mother Odessa cleaned and cooked for the upper-class whites in Louisville, however, mainly she was a mother to Ali and his brother Rahman. Though not materially rich in the way white middle-class families would expect to be, they did own their own house in an area distant from the poor black neighbourhood of Smoketown, and there was never a hint of Ali or his brother going without food or clothes, as did many black children of that era.

For a future Nation of Islam zealot, his earlier lineage throws up a few uncomfortable truths. Despite later claiming that his birth name was a slave name, there was in fact a good deal of pride about it within the family.

Ali with his mum, Odessa – 'a sweet, fat, wonderful woman'.

Cassius Clay was actually named after a nineteenth-century Kentucky plantation owner, who in his later life became an abolitionist and one of the first men in the state to free his slaves. Ali was also of mixed blood, and again, despite claiming that this was the result of rape, the actual truth is that one of his mother's grandfathers was Tom Moorehead, the result of an entirely consensual union between a white man and a slave named Dinah, and the other was Abe

Grady, a Irish immigrant from County Clare who married a black woman. He may have changed his slave name later, but for now he wore it with a fair degree of pride.

His mother, Odessa Clay, was a devout woman, from whom Ali inherited his deep well of spirituality, with a keen sense of family and a warm heart. In Thomas Hauser's biography Ali remembers her fondly: 'She's a sweet, fat, wonderful woman, who loves to cook, eat, make clothes, and be with family.'

Muhammad and the family Clay: brother Rahman, mother Odessa and father Cassius Snr.

His relationship with his father was more complex. David Remnick, editor of *The New Yorker* and author of a book about Ali called *King of the World*, describes Cassius Clay Senior as 'a cock of the walk, a braggart, a charmer, a performer, a man full of fantastical tales and hundred-proof blather'.

Despite being an obvious chip off the block, Ali was very guarded when asked about his father, probably because Cassius Senior was also a violent drunk who assaulted his mother, was arrested many times, as well as being an inveterate womaniser who further humiliated Odessa with his habit of spending nights moving from bar to bar picking up women.

This chaotic and frightening aspect of an otherwise tightly knit and relatively comfortable family life must have had an effect on Ali. Interestingly, Remnick quotes one of Ali's closest friends, who believed that this aspect of his upbringing had a deforming affect on Ali's development: 'In many ways, as brilliant and charming as he is, Muhammad is an arrested adolescent. There is a lot of pain there . . . a lot of that pain comes from his father, the drinking, the occasional violence, the harangues.'

But Cassius Clay Senior was no hopeless dissolute. He

was a hard-working man who provided well for his family. But like many black men of his generation, he was resentful and full of anger. He believed the white man had kept him down, ensured he remained a sign painter not able to fulfil his ambition to be a proper painter of landscapes and religious themes. Whatever the truth of this feeling, he passed on to Ali a strong sense of the need for black self-determination. A sense compounded by the second influential strand of his childhood – namely, the society that he grew up in.

Ali was born and grew up in a segregated society. In the more 'enlightened' Northern states, where the so-called 'Jim Crow' laws of racial segregation had been repealed, segregation ran along economic and social lines, where job discrimination, unfair labour practices and housing policies

‘Muhammad Ali was important because he was self-possessed in the best sort of way . . . he was a powerful influence on many lives. Because of him, people became convinced that if they stood up for their beliefs, they could prevail.’

Bill Bradley, American former
basketball player and politician

created black ghettoes in the poorer parts of the cities. In the South, the former Confederate States still operated and enforced the laws governing the implementation and maintenance of racial segregation. Louisville was in Kentucky. Kentucky was a Jim Crow state.

It is difficult from the perspective of a white European man to understand what Ali experienced every day of his childhood. If he strayed outside his neighbourhood into a white one he would quickly hear the calls of 'Nigger' and 'Nigger go home'. All around him was evidence that he was, because of the colour of his skin, a second-class citizen. There were separate white and black public facilities, schools and stores. In the cinemas, the whites sat in the stalls, the blacks in the balcony. He would watch and be affected by the daily humiliations heaped upon his mother and father because of the colour of their skin. It is a fact that Ali had certain advantages over other black children, but he was still denied the basic liberties that any human warranted.

But it was the murder of a fourteen-year-old boy named Emmett Till in 1955 that most vividly and frighteningly brought home to Ali where he stood in the world and what he could expect. Emmett Till, a black boy from Chicago, was holidaying with relatives in Mississippi. He was with a group of friends and he was boasting about his non-segregated school in Chicago, and showing round a picture of his white girlfriend. As a dare, one of his friends pointed to a store with a white cashier and said he should go and speak to her. Not realising the danger he was in, Emmett walked into the store, talked a while and left saying 'Bye, baby.' This was the Deep South. Negroes were not just second-class citizens, they were subhuman. The next night the cashier's husband and his brother-in-law abducted Till from the house he was staying at, beat him, shot him in the head and weighed his body down in the Tallahatchtie River by tying barbed wire around his neck and attaching a ceiling fan to it. The two men were arrested but the all-white jury acquitted both of them after being told by the Defense lawyer that their 'forebears would turn in their graves' if they convicted the defendants, Roy Bryant and J. W. Milman. It took them just over an hour. One explained it took them that long because they spent some of the time drinking lemonade.

This event was the final straw for the black community, giving powerful impetus to the civil rights movement, and opening Ali's eyes clearly to what lay ahead for him. His father made sure Ali was aware of every detail of the case, even showing him pictures in the press of Till's mutilated body. Here was a boy a year older than him, killed because he winked at a white woman. All Ali could see was that he was going out into a world that would hate and rebuff him at every turn. It was a formative experience.

The final strand that would leave a less obvious but no less important mark on Ali was his experience at school. He entered high school in 1957, but his grades were so poor that he had to withdraw and come back the next year to start again. He finally graduated as number 371 out of a graduation class of 391, and was given an IQ of 83, which puts him in a group defined as having low intelligence. Part of the reason for this could be that by now he had devoted himself entirely to boxing and spent most of the time in school declaring he was 'the greatest' whilst shadow-boxing down the school corridors. But it was also clear that he struggled with his studies not merely because of a lack of application but also because of a difficulty in reading and processing information.

What's confusing about this picture is that his academic performance is totally at odds with his nature. His parents remembered him as an inquisitive child with an enquiring mind and a quicksilver tongue who questioned all that he saw around him and who understood at a very young age the basic unfairness of the society he grew up in. This is not the profile of a boy who was a dunce, but perhaps of one who had a learning difficulty. Indeed his last wife Lonnie believes that he may have suffered from undiagnosed dyslexia. Too much could be made of this – and there is no evidence to suggest that Ali was troubled by this at the time; he was probably too busy dreaming of becoming the world champion – but there is no doubt that he left school with a basic education, an untrained mind, and with the kind of labelling that leaves a mark in a young person, a small bubble of insecurity and inferiority. This mental scar would crucially inform the way he behaved when the draft board came calling or when a certain interviewer asked him to read a passage from a book! It also made him vulnerable to the kind of neat 'tied in a bow' solutions and theories that movements like the Nation of Islam peddled to explain difficult and complex issues like racial discrimination.

'To all intents and purposes, Cassius Clay was born at the age of twelve, the day he entered a boxing gym.'

Wilfred Sheed, novelist and critic

The story of Ali, the boxer, began one night in Louisville, Kentucky, when a twelve-year-old boy went to retrieve his beloved red and white Schwinn bike after a night out with his friend at a fair held at the Columbia Auditorium. The bike had gone, and whoever had stolen it was going to get a good whuppin'.

In tears at his loss, he was told that there was a policeman who had a boxing gym in the basement of the auditorium and that he should go and see him. The policeman was Joe Martin and he suggested to Ali that if he was intent on revenge, perhaps he might want to learn how to throw a punch first.

Ali with Joe Martin, his first boxing coach. Getting ready to give the bike thief a good whuppin'.

For Martin, what initially set Ali apart from other kids was his commitment and discipline. He would run four or five miles every morning before school. He would train at the gym long after his contemporaries had gone home. He would talk about his body being a temple, watch what he would eat. Boxing for him became all-consuming, and he began to make a name for himself on the amateur boxing programme called *Tomorrow's Champions*, which Martin produced for the local NBC affiliate channel.

As he learned to box, his innate talent shone through as he developed his unique style: circling the ring up on his toes, the hands hanging low, the snaking left jab. Martin immediately saw that he had an uncanny ability to avoid being hit, an eerie way that his eyes never seem to blink. He was also precocious in the way he read a fight, the way he dealt with a crisis. 'When he'd get hit he wouldn't get mad and wade in, the way some boys do. He'd take a good punch and then he'd go right back to boxing.'

He was, it seems, a natural-born boxer, and even then he would tell his classmates he would be the greatest of all time. This wasn't an empty boast; he was serious.

By the time he was eighteen he had an amateur record of one hundred wins and only eight losses, two National Golden Gloves championships and two National Amateur

Athletic Union titles. He had also started talking. He might have claimed on the *Parkinson* show that it was the wrestler Gorgeous George who first gave him the idea of how to sell tickets, but as a twelve year old he was mouthing off on television, making predictions, insulting the opposition. The more he did, the more the crowd used to bay, 'Button his lip!' 'Bash his nose in!' Even at this stage he knew exactly what he was doing, as he remembers in Thomas Hauser's book. 'I didn't care what they said as long as they kept coming to see me fight. They paid their money, they were entitled to a little fun.'

But this precocious talent was also in a rush. Sure of his destiny, full of self-belief. One night in 1957, Angelo Dundee, already one of the most respected trainers in boxing, was sitting in a hotel room in Louisville with his well-regarded light heavyweight Willie Pastrano. The phone rang and a fifteen-year-old boy said, 'I'm Cassius Marcellus Clay and I'm the Golden Gloves champion and I'm going to win the Olympic gold medal.' Intrigued to see this mad kid in the flesh, Dundee invited him up, and for the next couple of hours Ali quizzed him about boxing. A couple of years later, Dundee saw that the kid was more than just talk. At seventeen he convinced Angelo to let him spar with Pastrano, the then world champion. After two rounds where Pastrano flailed around whilst Ali danced and hit him at will, Dundee pulled his fighter out of the ring. He knew he had seen something special, so when the call came later for him to train Ali, it was an easy decision.

Despite, in his own head, being the biggest thing in boxing, Ali was still virtually unknown as a fighter. The Rome Olympics in 1960 changed all that but, like most things with Ali, there was a twist in the tail. Ali was terrified of flying. So much so that he looked at all manner of alternative transport options. When he realised that flying was the only realistic means of getting to the Olympics, he decided that he did not need to go anyway: he would become the greatest without winning a gold medal. It was only after a lengthy meeting with Joe Martin that Ali was persuaded to go, but not without taking some precautions first. Before the flight, Ali visited an army surplus store and purchased a parachute, which he strapped to his back for the duration of the flight. His fear of flying was the hardest opponent he had to overcome at the Games. He sailed though the rounds to win gold, dazzling observers with his boxing skill and charming everyone and anyone in the Olympic Village.

When he returned from Rome the world was at his feet. He was handsome, gifted, witty and entertaining and, more importantly, he loved his country. When asked by a Soviet

Winning gold at the 1960 Rome Olympics.

reporter about his feelings on winning a gold medal for a country that had restaurants he couldn't eat in, Ali declared, 'To me the USA is the best country in the world, including yours. It may be hard to get something to eat sometimes, but anyhow I ain't fighting alligators and living in a mud hut.' It was a comment printed in many US newspapers as evidence of his good citizenship.

At this stage Ali, though aware that his gold medal had changed little about Louisville, was a long way from being the public face of the segregationist Nation of Islam. In

1960 he had deep concerns about the racial divide in America, but the closest he had come to being an activist was when he had attended a civil rights march in the late 1950s and got soaked by water thrown by a white woman. His reaction was to declare that 'this was the last one of these I'm coming to', He simply wanted to earn enough money to buy a nice house for his parents, and one for himself, to settle down and raise kids. On top of that he wanted to be the greatest heavyweight champion the world had ever seen, and he wanted to do it in double-quick time so he could retire while he was still pretty.

He was hot property and he knew it. He quickly declared he was turning pro and sat back and waited for the offers of management. Ten or fifteen years earlier, Ali would have been taken to lunch by a *capo* from the Cosa Nostra and made an offer he couldn't refuse. In 1960 things were different. Bobby Kennedy had begun his war on the Mob and they were fighting too many internal fires to keep their stranglehold on the fight game. Ali was also helped by his middle-class upbringing and abstemious tendencies, which meant he would never be like a Sonny Liston or Floyd Patterson, whose dysfunctional, desperately poor upbringings could easily lead to a life of crime or substance abuse, which would then lead neatly in to the arms of the

Mob. Ali would therefore be the first high-profile boxer since the turn of the century to choose his own manager.

His first managers were the Louisville Sporting Group, an all-white group of rich men from old-money Kentucky families who clubbed together to help out a well-behaved Kentucky boy with whom they could have a bit of fun and perhaps earn some money. It was, as David Remnick put it, 'an adventure in Jim Crow paternalism'. To be fair, the deal they did with him was both generous and far-sighted. Along with a $10,000 signing-on fee, he was guaranteed over $4,000 a year for the first two years and 35 per cent of his earnings would be placed in a pension that he could not touch until he was thirty-five.

But if his management thought he'd be a well-behaved and grateful Louisville black boy, they were in for a shock. Ali's outspokenness and refusal to listen resulted in a split with his first trainer, Archie Moore. Moore wanted to change Ali's style but Ali was having none of it. Moore wanted him to go hard early on, get the opponent out of there as quickly as possible, protect his body from too many hard fights. Ali wanted to dance, to box like Sugar Ray, to float like a butterfly and sting like a bee. Given the fights that were to come, perhaps he should have paid more attention to his trainer. The Louisville Sporting Group suggested to Moore that perhaps what Ali needed was 'a good spanking'. Moore agreed, but wondered who'd be able to give it to him.

Angelo Dundee was the next candidate as trainer, and he was the perfect fit for Ali. In the trainer/fighter relationship, Dundee saw himself as second banana; this suited Ali, who never wanted to be controlled. Dundee could also see that he had to work with what was in front of him and not try to change him.

'For a hundred years, the only thing fighters would say was, "I do the fighting; my manager does the talking." But then Muhammad came along, saying, "Hey, I do the talking. I'm the star. Nobody else talks for me."'

A seemingly tricky assignment for any manager, never mind someone as gifted as Dundee, was made easier by the fact that Ali was a dream fighter to work with – a teetotaller with iron self-discipline, who loved to train but who was also blessed with great natural advantages. Ferdie Pacheco, who became Ali's physician and worked alongside Dundee, observed at the time: 'If someone came from another planet and said, "Give us your best specimen", you'd give him Ali. Perfectly proportioned, handsome, lightning reflexes and a great mind for sports.'

Ali was totally self-aware, even at twenty-one. He knew exactly where he was going and how he'd get there. He

Angelo Dundee with Ali. 'I didn't train Ali, I directed him and made him feel like he was the innovator.'

said at the time, 'Where do you think I be next week if I wasn't shouting and hollering and making the people take notice? I'd be poor and in my hometown . . . saying "yussuh" and "nawsuh" and knowing my place.'

The Louisville Lip had been born and no one was going to button it. Using his golden boxing skill and silver-tongued charm, he took the fight game by storm, became the darling of the press and the public, and was having a great time doing it. As Pacheco remembers, 'Everything was such fun to him . . . No one shut him up. So he just kept predicting and winning, predicting and winning. It was like in *Candide*: he didn't think anything could happen in the best of all possible worlds.'

But this is where the story becomes more complex. If, on the surface, he was having fun being in complete control of his destiny, with each new piece of showboating, no matter how outrageous, being another step in his inevitable journey to the heavyweight crown, inside he was in turmoil. It was no surprise. Ali, the tub-thumping, cocky self-publicist was troubled by his conscience and pricked by the lessons drummed into him as a kid by his father about the need for black self-determination and black pride. Lessons made flesh by growing up in this period of civil rights violations that were proving the depth and savagery of white racism. Yet here he was making his name in a sport that – as David Remnick pointed out in *King of the World* – had its origins in slavery. Plantation owners would pit their strongest slaves against each other in a form of human dog fighting, with the slaves wearing iron collars and often fighting to the point of death. Ali would sometime later ask a room full of white reporters why a bunch of white guys had come to watch two black boys beat each other up. It wasn't a throwaway line; it reflected his deep misgivings about the spectacle of two black men fighting in a country that denied them basic rights.

On top of this, Ali would also be expected – as a black fighter and future world champion – to defer to white sensibilities. To keep his mouth shut. He should not in any way use his status in the black community to become involved in the social and political upheaval that was going on around him. Ali was never going to be comfortable with this. His upbringing and early life had not yet radicalised him, but it had made him wary and resentful of the white man, which in turn informed his anti-authoritarian nature and determination to forge his own path without the help or permission of the white ruling class. He was a conflicted and confused young man, and he went in search of answers to the difficult questions raised by his early experiences and his chosen career.

Since he had returned from the Olympics, he had become increasingly interested in the burgeoning civil rights movement. He attended meetings of various organisations, but it was the Nation of Islam that caught his imagination. The problem was that his interest in a movement that was anathema to most of white America had to remain a secret if he wanted a world title shot. So whilst he went about whupping all comers in the ring, and the media into a frenzy outside it, he was at the same time concealing from the outside world his inner life and his gradual conversion to Islam through the teachings of Elijah Muhammad.

Elijah Muhammad had taken over leadership of the Nation of Islam from its founder Wallace Fard Muhammad, who had established the organisation in 1930 to put black people 'on the road to self-independence with a superior culture and higher civilisation than they had previously experienced'. Elijah Muhammad claimed he was the messenger of Allah and had been sent to preach not only that black men were the original Muslims, but also that they would inherit the earth. It rested upon a story of a large-headed man called Mr Yaccub who was born 6,600 years ago and as revenge for being exiled from the ancient city of Mecca, the home of the original righteous black man, created a race of blue-eyed, blond-haired devils that in turn enslaved the black men.

In reality, the Nation of Islam at this time behaved like a cult with a racially motivated political programme. It used a religious narrative and a charismatic, semi-divine leader to lend historical weight and justification to its message and to exert itself over its believers. In the case

Elijah Muhammad, leader of the Nation of Islam and one of the few men Ali ever listened to.

of the Nation of Islam, the message was the racial supremacy of the black man and the need for complete segregation from the white man. It was such a racist message that it actually got approval from the KKK, who preached their own brand of racial purity.

The question is: why did Ali choose this particular message? He didn't in his normal life seem to hate white people. He was managed by a group of them and had two more in his corner. It seemed to go against his natural character and instincts, which were inclusive and open. His father would later claim he had been brainwashed. That could be more the reaction of an estranged parent than an opinion based on fact, but it is certainly a modus operandi of cults down the years, and Ali – with his minimal education and perhaps a lack of discernment – could have been vulnerable to this kind of movement. He was also a deeply spiritual man who would go nowhere without his Bible, often asking God at a young age to send him a sign to show him his purpose as a black man in a country that hated him. He was in many ways ripe for conversion to a religion and belief system that neatly placed black men at the centre of the universe. Was Elijah Muhammad the sign he had been waiting for?

Some members were not averse to coercive and controlling behaviour. In later years they were accused of driving a wedge between Ali and his family, and convincing him to divorce his first wife, Sonji. They were also known to use strong-arm tactics to deter disbelievers and critics. Some were reformed ex-cons, and unfavourable reports by journalists were often followed by death threats.

Also, I believe, his strong sense of the need to bring black pride back to his people meant he was attracted to a religion and a movement that gave back self-worth and self-esteem to the black man. Even the integrationist civil rights movements, which worried about the confrontational approach of these black Muslims, admired the way they rehabilitated men coming out of prison, preached morality in the home and on the street. Ali never forgot the humiliations of his parents, the casual racism of the community he grew up in, the feeling of being downtrodden. The Nation of Islam gave them hope. In the words of Louis Farrakhan, Elijah Muhammad's right-hand man: 'Elijah Muhammad took the dope needle out of our arms . . . took the wine bottle out of our hands . . . stopped us from throwing our money away on horse races and gambling. And he told us, Pool that money, brother. Pool that money, sister. And let's do constructive things.'

It also provided Ali with a family. In Elijah Muhammad he got the father figure he had yearned for. A figure who could replace his natural father's bitter and angry harangues about the black man's fate with a vision that gave Ali hope, one that put black men front and centre of the world stage. In Malcolm X, who was a key character within the Nation of Islam, Ali got the elder brother who both inspired and educated. This leading light of the movement had genuine affection for Ali and, seeing his hunger for knowledge, used his powerful rhetorical skill to teach him that the way forward was not to beg or negotiate for their freedoms, but to take back what was naturally theirs by any means necessary. Peaceful marches, sit-ins, integrationist policies were not the solution. Segregation and collective action as a race in the name of Allah to better things for themselves was the way. Moreover, if Ali accepted the teachings of Elijah, he would be invincible. Allah would be in his corner. This heady mix of creed and personality drew Ali towards it like a moth to a flame. For Malcolm X it presented the chance to lend real legitimacy to the movement by turning the greatest fighter the world had ever seen into a Holy Warrior for the Nation of Islam cause.

While he wrestled with his conscience and inner beliefs, his boxing career was blossoming. Beating all comers, often predicting the round in which they would fall, ensuring the world knew he was 'the greatest', attracting huge audiences to all of his fights, and creating a profile in the boxing world that allowed him to go 'bear hunting', the 'bear' being the heavyweight champion of the world, the ferocious, indestructible, unbeatable Sonny Liston.

Liston was not a man to mess with. Possibly the most destructive, dangerous and malignant heavyweight ever, he was possessed of immense power and a nasty streak a mile wide. He was owned by the Mob, who used him as an enforcer. His stare was enough to make most opponents wither before the first bell.

Although intimations of Ali's involvement with the Nation were coming out in the press in dribs and drabs, Ali was guarded and careful about any questions relating to race and, anyway, it was Ali's mental state that was most concerning journalists and fans alike. Mainly because, as Ali piled up victories, enhancing his reputation with every bout, he began a concerted campaign of trying to bait Liston into fighting him.

On one occasion he even travelled a thousand miles in a bus to stand outside Liston's home waving placards about giving him a whuppin', until Liston came outside and threatened serious damage if Ali and his party didn't get off his lawn. The world looked on and wondered but, like everything Ali did, there was method in his madness. He was afraid of what Liston could do if he came to the ring in the right frame of mind. So, rather like the time he let another behemoth punch himself out, he wanted to discombobulate Liston so that he wouldn't be thinking straight when they came face to face in the ring.

If the press and public thought that was mad, then it was nothing compared to the antics he got up to when the fight was finally set for 25 February 1964 in the Miami Convention Hall. Then, bear-baiting began in earnest: following Liston in his car, insulting him whilst he played craps in a Las Vegas Hotel, reciting poetry about how the fight would end. But it was Ali's performance at the weigh-in that really got people talking. He entered wide-eyed, shouting at the top of his voice about how he was going to give Liston a 'whuppin'', lunging at the champion and convincing everyone there that he was either having a nervous breakdown or was just plain scared. It was a performance that earned him a $2,500 fine from the boxing authorities and the conviction of every journalist present that he was unstable and unfit to fight. But the only person's opinion Ali cared about was Liston's; for his part, Liston was deeply unsettled, convinced he was about to face a deranged opponent. It was pure Ali. Theatrical, psychological warfare.

Despite being a rank outsider to whom no one gave a chance, Ali out-boxed Liston, who didn't come out for the seventh round. At the age of twenty-two, Ali was the world champion. He stood on the ropes and screamed at the assembled journalists to, 'Eat your words.' But the world didn't seem that hungry.

For many it was a tarnished victory and the capitulation of Liston stank. Ali was too young, Liston a monster, it was a mismatch. But the odds on an Ali upset were huge, and Liston was also mobbed up, prepared to do his masters' bidding, even if that meant throwing a fight. Ali's camp countered that Liston was on the ropes, out-boxed, cut below the eye. They would cite the incident where Liston's camp tried to even the playing field. During the fourth round, with Ali way ahead on points and Liston swinging at air, an anticoagulant applied to his cut somehow found its way on to Liston's gloves and into Ali's eyes, meaning Ali fought much of the fifth round 'blind'. Whatever the truth, and to this day nothing has been proved, a rematch was ordered, but not before Ali changed before the audience's eyes. In the post-fight press conference, an unusually subdued Ali laid out his vision for the future. 'I only fight to make a living, and when I have enough money, I won't fight any more.' Crucially, he was then asked if he was a card-carrying member of the black Muslims – an umbrella term used by much of the media at the time – and the cat was out of the bag. 'I believe in Allah and I believe in peace. I don't try to move into white neighbourhoods. I don't want to be marrying a white woman.'

It was not that surprising an admission, because in the run-up to the fight the speculation about Ali joining the 'black Muslims' had reached a crescendo, particularly because of the presence at Ali's training camp and in his entourage of Malcolm X. Interestingly, Malcolm's presence was in fact not as a disciple of Elijah Muhammad, but as Ali's friend and 'confessor'. Malcolm had fallen out with Elijah and had been suspended as a member of the Nation of Islam. Elijah, for his part, was uninterested in Ali at this stage. He saw boxing as degrading to black men, and was also convinced Ali would lose; he didn't want one of his so-called followers to disgrace his movement by getting bashed up in the ring by a 'white man's nigger'.

The aftermath of Ali's admission, was one of the darkest periods in Ali's life and probably the most formative. His father was enraged, publicly denouncing black Muslims

Ali's friend and confessor Malcolm X.

as conmen and brainwashers. The press corps turned against him to a man, and white America was outraged, bewildered and concerned.

Even black commentators and activists were ambivalent in their support for a man they had held in high esteem, but now saw as a real threat to their pursuit of integration and equal rights because of his support for such a confrontational and uncompromising credo. Ali was most hurt by the condemnation of his childhood hero Joe Louis. 'Clay will earn the public's hatred because of his connections with the black Muslims,' he said.

In fact the only support he did get was from the segregationist senator for Georgia, Richard Russell, who saw a kindred spirit, and, not surprisingly, Elijah Muhammad who, knowing a good thing when he saw it, conquered his distaste for boxing and publicly welcomed Ali into the Nation of Islam fold, declaring the fight had been a victory for Allah.

Ali reacted to this outpouring of condemnation in the only way he knew. He came out fighting. In every public utterance from now until the next Liston fight, he refused to back down, confirming with his trademark passion and poetic, street-preacher fluency his conversion to Islam, if not yet the full belief system of the Nation of Islam.

'I ain't no Christian. I can't be, when I see all the coloured people fighting for forced integration getting blown up . . . I don't want to be blown up. I don't want to be washed down sewers. I just want to be happy with my own kind . . .

'People brand us a hate group . . . That is not true . . . All they [followers of Allah] want to do is live in peace . . . I like white people. I like my own people. They can live together without infringing on each other.'

What turned him into a mouthpiece for the Nation and the espouser of the full belief structure of the movement was the choice he had to make between his surrogate father and brother, Elijah Muhammad and Malcolm X. Ali's public conversion to Islam coincided with a bitter power struggle between the two as they fought for control of the movement. The problems stemmed from the fact that Malcolm couldn't equate the clean-living Islamic creed of the messenger with Elijah's financial impropriety and desire for young women. He was also beginning to question the basis of the Nation's creed, and indeed its segregationist solution to the race issue. Elijah, who had saved this former drug runner and street hoodlum from a life in prison, now saw his protégé, chief recruiter and most charismatic, intelligent and eloquent of preachers as a threat. He had already banned Malcolm from the movement in a bid to censure and control him, and now Ali became a pawn in a latter-day *Game of Thrones*.

After the Liston fight, Malcolm took Ali to New York, where they both held court. In response Elijah held a press conference, where he declared that Cassius Clay was no more and that he was now Muhammad Ali. The significance of this was not lost on Malcolm. Normally new recruits would take the second name of X, with the full Islamic moniker reserved until they had become long-term and trusted converts. In bestowing the full Islamic name immediately, Elijah was sending out a clear message. He wanted Ali's loyalty in his war with Malcolm. He also wanted Ali as the Nation's cash cow and chief recruiter.

Ali was now faced with a simple choice between Elijah and Malcolm. Between loyalty to a man he saw as a messenger of God, who held the fate of the black man in his hands, and loyalty to a man he loved as a brother but would take him down a different path, away from the brotherhood. Ali chose Elijah, cutting ties with his friend and confidant, the man who had done most to convince him that Allah was in his corner.

It was done without much soul-searching, in a dismissive, almost cruel fashion. Ali simply cut Malcolm dead. It might seem odd from a white European perspective to choose a cult over a man who – in a crisis of conscience – had questioned the integrity of a movement and had come to a more logical and humane conclusion. But again, we can't view Ali through that prism. One cannot underestimate the level of Ali's blind faith; his belief that if he went with Malcolm he would be committing heresy. Nor would Malcolm's decision to seek integration with the white man sit comfortably with Ali. His strong sense of race was such that he didn't feel much like coming to any accommodation with the white man. He *was* the greatest; he would bow the knee to no one. It is also the case that a lot of pressure was being brought to bear on Ali, by members of the movement, to make the 'right' choice.

Cut adrift, Malcolm was living on borrowed time. He was assassinated in 1965 by two members of the Nation of Islam. Elijah Muhammad claimed they acted alone, but in the same way that Henry II, some 800 years earlier, had wondered aloud about ridding himself of his meddlesome priest, Elijah had made it quite clear that Malcolm X, by his rejection of his teachings, had placed himself in harm's way. It was also in 1965 that Ali knocked out Liston in the first round of their rematch and emerged as a fully fledged holy warrior and chief recruiter for the Nation of Islam, with the full weight of the black Muslim brotherhood behind and around him.

Their support of Ali quickly became a stranglehold. Many believed the brotherhood had fixed the second fight so that there was no chance their chief fundraiser and recruiter could lose. The rumours were that Liston had taken a fall, victim of a 'phantom punch' that no one had seen land. More rational observers, such as veteran boxing commentator Larry Merchant, saw it clearly, though. 'I saw the actual punch land on the actual chin, as did others in my area of the press section. It was a quick right hand that caught Liston as he was coming forward . . . According to ringside doctors I've spoken to, that is a classic example of a medulla-oblongata K.O.'

Whatever the truth, it was a fact that Ali was now central to black Muslims' advancement and in turn he became more reliant and dependent on them. As Cassius Senior's anger at his son's conversion led to a rift, they became his only family, and Elijah his adoptive father.

His entourage now featured more and more well-groomed, bow-tied, stern and uncompromising brothers, including Herbert Muhammad, Elijah's son, who would go on to become Ali's manager. They set about polishing their rough diamond. He was being educated, inculcated, indoctrinated with all the facets of their belief systems, which eventually led to a heartbroken Ali, supported and encouraged by the brothers, reluctantly parting with his first wife Sonji in 1966, after only two years of marriage, because of a personality and dress sense that did not sit well with the sensibilities of the Nation of Islam followers and the teachings of the Koran.

His language and views began to take on an uncompromising and unpleasant tone, defined by the narrow beliefs of the Nation of Islam. Here he is, in an interview with *Playboy* soon after his divorce. He was asked: "'What if a Muslim woman wants to go out with non-Muslim blacks – or white men for that matter?" Ali replied: "Then she dies. Kill her too.'"

All this took place in the febrile atmosphere of the Los Angeles Watts riots of August 1965, which left thirty-five dead and caused $40 milliom worth of damage, while President Johnson was trying to force the Civil Rights Bill through Congress. The Nation of Islam and its message of Black Power had taken centre stage, with Ali as its avenging angel.

He defended his title nine times, until he was banned in 1967 laying waste to four white challengers, including a second bout with Henry Cooper. This period saw the high-water mark of him as a fighter in a three-round demolition of Cleveland Williams, which Hugh McIlvanney

Ali dismantles Cleveland Williams, 14 November 1966.

describes as 'the greatest demonstration of boxing virtuosity' he had ever seen; but it also saw the emergence of a cruel, vindictive streak in the way he sadistically toyed with the totally outclassed Floyd Patterson and Ernie Terrell. All in the name of Allah. Both had positioned themselves as the defenders of Christian America and called him by his slave name Clay. In 1964, Ali v. Liston had been White Hat v. Black Hat. In three short years, and in the eyes of the general populace, Ali had taken Liston's choice of headgear.

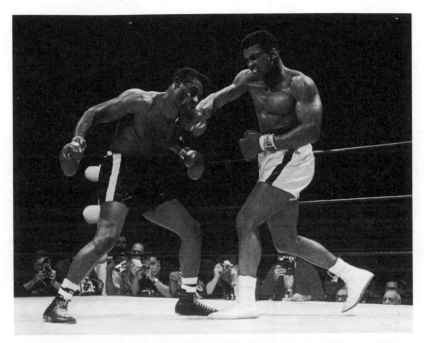

Floyd Patterson wishes he had called him Ali, 22 November 1965.

By the time he had humiliated Ernie Terrell in fifteen brutal rounds, during which Ali toyed with him like a cat with a dying mouse, punctuating every hurtful jab and slashing right with the question, 'What's my name?', he had had his passport confiscated by the US government for refusing the Vietnam draft. Ali had become public enemy number one.

Ali's complicated history with the draft board began in 1962, when he took the army induction tests and gained such a low mark that the army put his IQ at 78. This placed him in the lowest bracket the army had and made him ineligible for service. For Ali this was humiliating, a reminder of his struggles in high school, except this time the whole country knew about it. As he himself remembers, not only did he not know the answers, he didn't understand the questions. Trying to laugh it off he quipped, 'I said I was the greatest, not the smartest.' Further humiliation followed when, two months later, unable to believe that this motor-mouth world champ was that intellectually challenged, they retested him to make sure he wasn't faking his ignorance. He wasn't. Did it matter? Those around weren't concerned. As Ferdie Pacheco observed: 'Ali's army IQ score was 78. So what! Measuring Ali's intelligence with a standard IQ test is like trying to measure joy or love with a ruler.'

But this was 1966, and with the Vietnam War spreading in scope and increasing in intensity, the army began escalating its troop levels, and as a result needed the chaff as well as the wheat. Ali's score, deemed too low four years previously, was now good enough for active service.

Ali received the news at his house where he was relaxing with a few Muslim brothers and reporter Robert Lipsyte. The phone kept ringing, with journalists mischievously asking Ali complicated questions about the war. The fact is that the war wasn't on his radar screen, and the more Ali couldn't answer, the more he became frustrated. The atmosphere was not helped by the Muslim brothers goading him about what would happen to a black boy in the army. He finally snapped, and in answer to a question about the Viet Cong, Ali famously replied: 'Man, I ain't got no quarrel with the Viet Cong.' A statement born of anger and frustration. An off-the-cuff quip that reverberated around the world.

But like most times when his back was against the wall, Ali refused to give in, particularly when there was a point of principle at stake. Not even offers of a cushy deployment staging exhibition fights for the troops would dissuade him from refusing on religious grounds. 'I either have to obey the laws of the land or the laws of Allah. I have nothing to lose by standing up and following my beliefs. We've been in jail for four hundred years.'

Ali's refusal to accept the draft resulted in him being sentenced to five years in prison and a $10,000 fine. He was immediately banned from boxing and his title gifted to Jimmy Ellis who would go on to lose it in the ring to Joe Frazier. He would not fight again for three and a half years – the prime years of his boxing career taken from

Ali, the race warrior, talks segregation of the races. Martin Luther King listens and wonders, 'What if?'

him, his career, fame and livelihood sacrificed on a point of principle. But Ali had no regrets. 'I was determined to be the one nigger the white man didn't get.'

Ali spent his time in exile constantly living under the threat that his appeals against his conviction would fail and he would serve time. However, he also found time to remarry. This time to a good Muslim girl called Belinda. He also discovered that he could make money by appearing on the college lecture tour circuit. It was here that he honed his views on every aspect of his life, from the war in Vietnam, being stripped of his title, segregation, inter-marriage, the need for money – views which he would trot out verbatim on talk shows in later years. Delivered in his inimitable style he was a hit, mainly because the mood of the nation was changing. America was turning against the war, increasingly horrified by the returning body bags that contrasted starkly with the positive messages about the progress of the fighting being peddled by the government. Ali became a lightning rod around which the anti-war movement began to coalesce. He was, for all his divisive viewpoints, sincere. He had inadvertently tapped into the changing mood of the country.

His increasing appeal meant that his lectures were enjoyed by not only black students but white ones from

Middle America too, exposing them for the first time to the question of race, identity and the need for black pride as a basic issue of human rights and not merely a question of better race relations. He began to win back the hearts he had lost over his conversion to Islam and refusal of the draft. He made them laugh, made them think, and when he returned to fighting after his conviction was overturned unanimously in 1971, he invited them to join him on an odyssey to take back what was rightfully his.

But it was not going to be easy. Those three and a half years in exile would have been the peak years of Ali's boxing career. As Pacheco recalls, 'The world never saw what might have been. And that's very sad, like knowing a Mozart symphony or a play by Shakespeare was somehow censored out of existence.'

Pacheco, ever the wordsmith, was in essence correct. For a man who was blessed with a preternatural boxing talent, to have his peak years stripped from him was akin to a Shakespearean tragedy. Now Ali would never have the chance to show how 'great' he could have been. Perhaps, given this 'loss', it is understandable how Ali was so driven – and at times careless of his personal safety – in the coming years.

The biggest problem Ali faced was that, in the opinion of Dundee and Pacheco, his legs had gone, and with them his first line of defence, the thing that made him so difficult to hit. Sadly, in the light of what came later, he then discovered he had an ability to take a punch, to take incredible punishment to the head and body. Before the break he would train by not letting anyone hit him; now he let the sparring partners go at him to toughen his body, whilst Pacheco winced at every strike to his kidneys. His hands were also a problem area. Like most fighters, he suffered with arthritis in the knuckle joints, and would for the remainder of his career need cortisone injections in his hand before each fight. The Ali post-exile would be a shrewder, more tactical fighter. The quicksilver, thrilling Ali had gone for ever.

But, like Jason before him, if he were to capture the Golden Fleece of the world championship belt, he would have to slay a few beasts first. Before his exile he had been at the top of the food chain, the predator in the boxing world. However, on his return, heavyweight boxing had entered the Jurassic age, where monsters ruled the earth. One of the biggest was Joe Frazier, the man who had had the temerity to wear the belt Ali believed was his alone.

If there was one fighter who defined and ultimately diminished Ali as a boxer, it was Frazier. Frazier and Ali were made for each other in more ways than one. Norman Mailer called Frazier 'a war machine'. He was the battering ram, Ali the rapier. Frazier came at his opponent in a low crouch, taking three shots to get two in, remorseless, indomitable and savage. His punches were fearsome and damaging and he could fell a man with either hand. Ali was upright, beautifully balanced, jabbing and weaving with a clear disdain for the cruder aspects of boxing. He fought with his head pulled back, as if being hit on the face was the ultimate insult. He didn't so much beat an opponent as show them how to dance.

In the shadowy world of heavyweight boxing, there are some encounters you can witness and come to the conclusion that one or the other fighter, for whatever reason, is not giving of his best. No one, not even the looniest conspiracy theorist, could watch the three Ali–Frazier fights without understanding that both fighters regarded each other with something approaching complete loathing.

Perhaps part of the reason for this was that outside the ring they were polar opposites who could never see eye to eye. Ali, the brash, polemical, Muslim race warrior from a comfortable background with the milk-chocolate looks, against the black-skinned, softly spoken, conformist, devout Baptist, twelfth child of a poverty-stricken sharecropper who peddled bootleg alcohol on the side. Ali, with his looks and his showmanship, had danced his way through life; Frazier had slugged it out in working boots. It was *Guess Who's Coming to Dinner?* If Sidney Poitier or Ali walks through the door it's one thing. If Joe Frazier turns up, then it's going to be a different ending.

However, the bad blood between the two was for the most part created and nurtured by Ali but, by the end, was returned in equal measure by Frazier. Ali had always taunted opponents. He would create a grudge against them, parodying their looks and boxing talent. In the main it was a means whereby he psyched himself up and sold tickets. Occasionally, such as in the bouts with Patterson and Terrell, the animosity was driven by anger caused by a slur on his religion. With Frazier it went a step further. It became bullying, sadistic – a boy using a magnifying glass on a fly. Ali called him an Uncle Tom, a gorilla, ignorant. In fact Joe was the archetypal black person for whom Ali had claimed to be fighting, and yet Ali demeaned him at every turn, painting a picture that unfairly separated Joe Frazier from the support of the black community. He placed Joe in the role of an instrument of the white power structure, while portraying himself as the symbol of black pride and the anti-war movement. It was not a position that Frazier either espoused or supported, but it was a role that Ali made sure he was cast in. The insults cut deeply with Smokin' Joe, and he had neither the verbal dexterity nor the political grounding to fight back. It was also doubly galling to be called an Uncle Tom by a man who was neither black like him nor minded having a significant number of people in his camp who were white. What incensed Frazier was Ali posturing as a representative of the downtrodden black man. Portraying himself as fighting 'for the little man in the ghetto', threatening to give Frazier 'a ghetto whuppin'', Frazier retorted, 'What does *he* know about the ghetto?'

The fact is a man as proud as Ali would have been angry with anyone who held the belt he still thought of as his when he returned to the ring. In Ali's view they had won it by default, without meeting him in the ring, and so became an object of disdain, not worthy of his respect.

Then Ali would begin a sustained campaign to prove that they were not good enough either in or out of the ring. In the opinion of veteran black American journalist and broadcaster, Bryant Gumbel, Frazier was sadly a decent, honest man in the wrong place at the wrong time. 'In fact, one of the sad stories to be written about that era is that Joe Frazier never got his due as a man. In some ways, he symbolised what the black man's struggle was about far more than Ali. But it was Joe's misfortune to be cast as the opponent of a man who was champion of all good things.'

Ali burned with a messianic zeal to get back his lost crown. For three and a half years he had been deprived of his livelihood, his reason for being. For three and a half years he had watched and waited, and now no one was going to deny him.

Ali was in a hurry. Within five months of returning to the ring, and after only two bouts in which to get fighting fit, he took on Frazier at Madison Square Garden in the so-called 'Fight of the Century'. For once the hyperbole matched the event. Billed as boxer against slugger, Nureyev against a threshing machine, on 8 March 1971 the eyes of the world were focused on a small square of canvas in Madison Square Garden.

Ali v. Frazier, Superfight 1, 8 March 1971. The threshing machine v. Nureyev.

It was a brutal, mesmerising contest over fifteen rounds, with Ali absorbing more punishment than he had ever done in his professional fight career, even being knocked down with a left hook in the fifteenth round. Frazier won by a unanimous decision, but both men knew they had been in a fight. For Pacheco, Ali had not given himself enough time to get the rust out of his boxing and the toughness into his body.

For many commentators, this was the end. Red Smith wrote: 'If they fought a dozen times, Joe Frazier would whip Muhammad Ali a dozen times; and it would get easier as they went along.' Budd Schulberg, the American novelist, sportswriter, and winner of the Oscar for the screenplay for the film *On the Waterfront*, was ringside for the fight, and saw echoes of Ali's defeat in the famous scene he had written in the back of the taxi with Marlon Brando and Rod Steiger.

'"I could've been a contender." I remember writing that scene. The whole scene was in the first draft of *On the Waterfront*, and that line remained unchanged. It came out of the fight game. I'd known boxers all my life, and seen that feeling in so many of them . . . If . . . If . . . If. And, certainly, watching the first Ali–Frazier fight, I had those thoughts. Because the Ali who came back to fight Joe Frazier wasn't the Ali I'd seen before. Those three and half years they took away from him as a fighter were years when he would have been in his prime.'

Ali was written off. But as always he had his own script. Asked to comment on the fact that Joe had said he didn't think Ali wanted to fight him again, Ali replied: 'Oh how wrong he is.'

It would be another three punishing years before he reclaimed his crown, and in the process sowed the seeds of his eventual downfall. But before all this he had a date in a London studio with a young British interviewer.

Chapter 2

ROUND 1, PARKINSON, BBC TV CENTRE, LONDON

17 October 1971

Ali in his prime. A magnificent specimen.

Chapter 2

'Float like a butterfly, sting like a bee.
His hands can't hit what his eyes can't see.'

Muhammad Ali

THE build-up to my first interview with Ali created a predictable ballyhoo. One headline I remember was 'Perky Parky v. The Louisville Lip', and another, 'Will Ali KO Parky?'

Ali and his entourage had taken a complete floor at a London hotel. We sent our best researcher – John Fisher – to talk to him, but the security was unyielding and contact with Ali impossible. He had been brought to London by a group of businessmen and part of the deal was a visit to a company in North London; the management had an idea of somehow involving Ali in their business. We were told that, en route, Ali would 'pop in' to the BBC TV Centre for a chat. We pointed out the chat would last an hour or more and were told we'd see about that. It's not often an institution like the BBC gets excited about a visitor, but with Ali there was a palpable expectation surrounding his visit. The demand for tickets was exceptional. To accommodate every request would have meant doing the interview in the Royal Albert Hall. You could also measure the fame and attraction of a guest by the number of staff who found a reason to be in the studio when the guest arrived. They weren't all hanging from the rafters, but there were only a few gaps.

When he walked into the studio there was an audible gasp. He was magnificent. I can think of no better word to sum up the elegant athleticism of his figure, the power of his smile. I led him into the set and showed him his position. He tried to sit down but the chair wasn't big enough. We'd had the same problem with Orson Welles a couple of weeks before, so we knew the answer was Bill Cotton's chair. Bill was the head of BBC Light Entertainment and liked a big chair – a throne, really. When Ali had settled, I remember being fascinated by his hands. They were large, his clenched fist twice the size of mine, but his fingers were long and tapering, the sort you could imagine caressing a keyboard rather than doing damage to another man's ribs. But most impressive of all was the ease with which he absorbed the paraphernalia of broad-casting, the fussing and primping of make-up, getting the lighting right, the mikes in position. He relished every moment and, as I watched him, I came to realise how he loved television, how he embraced it, how he could barely wait for the show to begin: his show – not mine!

And, of course, he was brilliant. Mad, provocative; by turns foolish then wise. Sometimes so extreme that his views about black/white relations made you wince and recoil, and then, in the next moment, so witty and funny you wondered if you were talking to another man.

I'd watched some of his American shows, so occasionally knew what was coming. When he started listing how pretty and talented he was, he kept pausing and looking at me in a questioning manner. I knew he was waiting for me to say something like, 'I'm not going to disagree.' At which point he would reply: 'You ain't as dumb as you look.' I saw it coming, did my bit, and he delivered the knockout blow. I often wondered how the interview might have proceeded and how long our professional relationship might have lasted had I replied as John Lennon did. When Ali said, 'You ain't as dumb as you look', Lennon had replied, 'No. But you are!'

Edited transcript of interview

MICHAEL : I think one of the things undeniable about you, Muhammad, is that you've got this flair for publicity. You attract it. Have you always had this gift, going right back?

ALI : No. I trained for a fella named Duke Sabedong. He was a Hawaiian fighter and he was a giant, about six feet eight inches tall. I was due to fight him in Las Vegas and I was on a television show. Gorgeous George – a famous American wrestler – was there talking before myself and I came on after him. During the time he was being interviewed he was saying, 'I am the prettiest wrestler; I am great, look at my beautiful blond hair. If that bum even messes my hair up, I'll annihilate him.' He said, 'George, what if you lose?' 'If I lose, I'm catching the next jet out to Russia. I want everybody out there to know if I lose . . .' He just got mad, said, 'I'm sick and tired, I'm getting off of this show,' and he ran off the show.

I was so nervous, I said, 'Boy, he sure talks a lot!' I had to go to see what he would do. Would he win or would he lose? When Gorgeous George came down the aisle, he had these two blonde, beautiful girls carrying his robe so it wouldn't get dirty. Real conceited and arrogant. And I was there in astonishment, just twenty-one years old and nobody knew me yet – Olympic champ, but I hadn't started talking yet. And I looked at him, and I said, 'Boy, he needs a good whooping.' I just wanted the other man to give him a good whooping. And he reached over and he took a can of beer out of the fellow's hand, he was arguing with him, and threw it in his face, and messed the man's suit up. Later I found out this fella worked with the show, but the people didn't know. He got up to his opponent's corner before his opponent got into the ring, he took some deodorant and sprayed the fellow's corner. He won the first fall, he lost the second fall, he won the third. But when I saw all of those people come to see Gorgeous George get beat – and they all paid to get in, that's the thing – I said, 'This is a good idea!' And right away I started talking – 'I am the greatest! I am beautiful! If you talk jive, you'll fall in five. I cannot lose!' In America, they've got a little saying – they said, 'The nigger talks too much!' And we sold everything, they lined up for miles, coming to see me get beat. And I went to the bank laughing every time!

MICHAEL: Can I go back to your childhood? When you were a kid in Louisville, did you get involved in fist fights and things like that?

ALI: A couple. I can remember a couple of those fights when I ran, because it's kind of dangerous. One fellow was going for a rock and another one was picking a stick. There weren't no referees or no judges and I got out! I've been in a couple of scuffles, but not too many.

MICHAEL: Did you belong to a gang in those days when you were a kid, were you running with a gang?

ALI: No I didn't, I didn't run with a gang. I didn't have time. I was so wrapped up in boxing since I was twelve, I'd always go to the gymnasium every day at six o'clock, after school, and in the mornings I would run, looking forward to the future Golden Glove and Olympic tournaments. I had something to do which most kids really need – something they can look forward to, a goal or purpose to work towards, something to achieve. It keeps them out of trouble. At the age of twelve I always had a good boxing talent, I was good for my age, and we had a local TV show called *Tomorrow's Champions*. It comes on in Louisville, Kentucky every Saturday at six o'clock. Three bouts, two minute-round bouts, and I had about forty-five fights on this show. I was so busy I didn't have time to rely on the street gangs.

MICHAEL: When you were twelve and in your early teens, did you ever imagine yourself as being world champion?

ALI: Right, it happened one night when I heard Rocky Marciano – 1954, 1953 or sometime. He had beaten Walcott or somebody and I was in the rain on my bicycle, leaning over listening to a fellow's radio in the car. I got there too late and I heard the fellow saying, 'And still the heavyweight champion of the world, Rocky Marciano!' and all the noise. I rode off in the rain on my bicycle and I could just hear the man saying, at that time my name was

Cassius Clay – 'And still the heavyweight champion of the whole world, Cassius Clay!' I heard it as I rode off in the rain and I said to myself, 'The champion of the whole world can whoop every man in Russia, every man in America, every man in China, every man in Japan, every man in Europe, every man in America.' So I kept working until I did. I wanted not only to be champion of the whole world, but better than all of those before me.

MICHAEL: I'm not gonna argue with you.

ALI: Then you're not as dumb as you look!

Completely at ease in a televison studio, the BBC TV Centre, October 1971.

MICHAEL: Can I turn the conversation a little bit, because you're as much now a political figure as you are an athlete.

ALI: I don't call myself a political figure. I'm seeking the peace.

MICHAEL: But you're involved in a political struggle, in a power struggle between black and white, and you're a leading member of that. Can I ask you when you were first aware, when you were a child, of the differences between black and white?

ALI: No, I've got to get that thing straight, I'm not involved in a power struggle, I'm not between black and white. I'm involved, I would say, in a freedom struggle, d'you understand, I wouldn't say power struggle. We're not trying to get that type of power, to rule nobody. We're just trying to get out from under the legal rule.

MICHAEL: But what I asked you was when was your first recollection as a child of being a second-class citizen, being treated like one?

ALI: Second class? No, more sixteenth class. They used to always say you're a second-class citizen, I'd always say to my mother, 'Momma, how come we're second-class citizens?' The African can go where I can't go, the Chinese can go where I can't go in America, the Englishman – you can come into white America and set up businesses and do things I can't do, and the Puerto Rican, the Hawaiian, and just about everybody came before the black people, more respected . . . I'm not just a boxer, I do a lot of reading, a lot of studying, I ask questions, I go out travelling these countries and watch how their people live and I learn. And I always ask my mother, 'Say Mother, how come is everything white?' I say, 'Why is Jesus white with blond hair and blue eyes? Why is the Lord's Supper all white men?' Angels are white, Paul and Mary, even the angels. I said, 'Mother, when we die, do we go to heaven?' She said, 'Naturally we go to heaven.' I said, 'Well, what happened to all the black angels? They took the pictures?' I said, 'If the white folks was in heaven too, then the black angels were in the kitchen preparing the milk and honey.' She said, 'Listen, you quit saying that, boy!'

I was always curious, and I always wondered why I had to die and go to heaven. How come I couldn't have pretty cars and good money and nice homes now? Why do I have to wait till I die to get milk and honey? And I said, 'Momma, I don't want no milk and honey. I like steaks.'

So anyway, I was always curious, I always wondered why Tarzan is the king of the jungle in Africa – he was white. I saw this white man swinging round Africa with a diaper on hollering! And all the Africans, he's beating them up and breaking the lion's jaw, and here's Tarzan talking to the animals, and the Africans have been there for centuries and can't talk to the animals – only Tarzan is talking to the animals. I always wondered why Miss America was always white, with all the beautiful brown women in America – beautiful suntans, beautiful shapes, all types of complexions

– but she always was white. And Miss World was always white, and Miss Universe was always white.

And this was when I knew something was wrong. I won the Olympic gold medal in Rome, Italy. Olympic champion. The Russian standing right here, and the Pole right here. I'm defeating America's so-called threats and enemies – I'm standing so proud and I'd have whooped the world for America! I took my gold medal, thought I'd invented something. Said, 'Man, I know I'm gonna get my people's freedom, I'm the champion of the whole world, Olympic champion. I know I can eat downtown now.' And I went downtown, I had my big old medal on, and the restaurants at that time weren't integrated, black folks couldn't eat downtown. I sat down, and I said, 'A cup of coffee and a hot dog.' The lady said, 'We don't serve Negroes.' I was so mad I said, 'I don't eat 'em, either, just give me a cup of coffee and a hot dog!' I said, 'I'm the Olympic gold medal winner. Three days ago I fought for this country in Rome, I won the gold medal, and I'm gonna eat.' I heard her telling the manager, and he said he's got to go out. And I had to leave that restaurant in my home town; I'd just won a gold medal and couldn't eat downtown. I says something's wrong. And from then on I've been a Muslim.

MICHAEL: Yes, I was going to ask you if that's what attracted you to Islam?

ALI: The truth, the teachings of Elijah Muhammad about how black people's been brainwashed. How they've been taught to love white and hate black. We're robbed of our culture, we were robbed of our true history, so it left us a walking dead man. So when you've got black people in our white country and they don't know nothing about themselves, they don't speak the language, they're just mentally dead. And this is happening all over the world. But the first place that we'll rise will be the black people in America, and then the rest of them will. The white people at that time, if one had five slaves and his name was Jones, they would be called Jones's property. If you was auctioned off to Mr Smith, your name was Smith. Identifying you as property for certain masters. So now that I'm free, now that I'm no longer a slave, then I want a name of my ancestors – Muhammad Ali. We don't have our names, we don't speak our true Arabic language, we were robbed of Islam, our true religion, and we've been made deaf, dumb and blind. Elijah Muhammad was taught to teach us the truth that will free us. And I've been free ever since.

MICHAEL: The advice of Muhammad teaches separatism, that the blacks shall have their own, but can I ask you about that? Wouldn't it make more sense, cause less pain all round in the struggle, in this battle, if it was integration rather than separatism? I mean, why do you reject integration?

ALI: We don't hate nobody. But Elijah Muhammad teaches us the truth of God. He teaches us that God beautified the planet earth by separating everybody and different countries to themselves – Chinese are in China, Englishmen's in England, Puerto Ricans in Puerto Rico, Ethiopians in Ethiopia, Arabians in Arabia, Egyptians in Egypt. Americans took that country and installed us. You're gonna always have chaos and trouble. It's a savage country. I notice here the policemen don't carry guns and they do not hit people with sticks. In America they have two policemen watching each other, each has got a pistol, one's got a machine gun, one's got a shotgun – and two dogs. They prowl the streets day and night. It's crazy, you see. We've been there six hundred years and there ain't no peace between black and whites because the cultures are different, like Chinese and Mexicans cannot integrate. The music is different, the eating is different.

MICHAEL: But to get this sort of separate state, do you think it can be achieved bloodlessly, or do you think there will be a fight?

ALI: Well there won't be on our part. It's totally impossible for thirty million black people to be violent against a hundred and seventy million. We need a mental revolution, unity and coming together, and not physical. And another thing, when you say integration, it comes in a marriage

too, right. All in together. And I'm sure no one tells a white
person watching this show, or no intelligent white man in
his or her right white mind want black boys and black girls
marrying their white sons and daughters.

MICHAEL: I wouldn't object to that.

ALI: Well you wouldn't, but a lot of them would . . . I don't
see no black and white couples in England or America
walking around proud, holding their children.

MICHAEL: That's society's fault. We've got to educate people
round it.

ALI: Well life is too short for me to be raising hell for something like that, I'd rather go and be with my own. I have
a beautiful daughter, beautiful wife, they look like me, we're
all happy and I don't have no trouble. And I ain't that
much in love with no woman to go through all that hell.
Ain't no one woman that good. Do you understand?

MICHAEL: I understand, yeah. I do understand, but I think
it's sad.

ALI: It ain't sad cos I want my child to look like me. Every
intelligent person wants his child to look like him. I'm
sad because I wanna blot out my race and lose my beautiful identity? . . . You hate your people if you don't want
to stay who you are, you ashamed what God made you?
God didn't make no mistake when he made us all like we
were.

MICHAEL: I think that's a philosophy of despair. I really do.

ALI: Despair, there ain't no despair. There's no woman on this whole earth – not even a black woman in African countries can please me and cook for me and socialise and talk to me like my American black woman. It's just nature. You can do what you want, but it's nature to want to be with your own. I want to be with my own. I love my people. And it keeps me out of trouble.

MICHAEL: I believe you when you say that you don't hate anybody, but Elijah Muhammad has been on record – you must have been asked this many times – as saying that white men are devils. You don't believe that, do you?

ALI: Yeah, I believe everything he preached. I'm his number one, his main follower. And if the white man ain't the devil, well, remember that he's aiming at the history of the American. He never said anything about Europe or Sweden or Canada. America. And if you can prove he's not the devil, then he should get on the television and call the man a liar.

MICHAEL: Are you saying that every white man in America is a devil? John F. Kennedy, was he a devil?

ALI: Well, who am I to say?

MICHAEL: Do you think he was?

ALI: Who am I to say he was the devil? I'm not Elijah Muhammad. I've heard Elijah Muhammad say this – there are many white people who mean right and in their heart wanna do right, but if ten thousand rattlesnakes was coming down that aisle now and I had a door here I could shut and in the ten thousand, one thousand meant right, one thousand rattlesnakes didn't want to bite me, I knew they were good, should I let all these rattlesnakes come down hoping that that thousand get together and form a shield, or should I just close the door and stay safe? You understand? The Viet Cong are not all bad but America is still dropping bombs. So now I'm going to forget the four hundred years of lynching and killing and raping and depriving my people of freedom, justice and equality, and I'm gonna look at two or three white people who are trying to do right and don't see the other million trying to kill me? I'm not that big of a fool and I'm not gonna deny it . . . Now what am I gonna do, get up and tell you Elijah Muhammad was wrong when he said they're the devil? They have to prove they're not the devil. You cannot lynch and kill and rape and burn and castrate a man, rape his women, for four hundred years, enslave them and burn them and still mistreat them and go and say he's not the devil.

MICHAEL: Can I, you mention there at the beginning, Vietnam, and I'd like to talk to you now about what happened when you refused to join the forces. As you said, the black Muslim movement is in fact—

ALI: It's just Muslim, it's not black Muslim. That's the press. And the history of the Americans is to divide and conquer. We're white Muslims, brown Muslims, yellow Muslims, tan Muslims, red Muslims and black Muslims. The Islam's the same world over – there ain't no such thing as a black Muslim. That's why they try to cut us off, my brothers in the rest of the world, to divide us in America and make other Muslims think that we are not with them. We're all the same. I recognise them, they recognise me, I'm invited to all their homes all over the world, I'm invited to Muslim countries, and the first thing they ask me is, 'Why do you call yourself black Muslims?' But the press give us the word 'black Muslims' to cut us off from them.

MICHAEL: But you refused to go and fight in Vietnam. Was that because you disagreed with the war in Vietnam or because you disagree with fighting generally?

ALI: I believe in the Holy Koran. It says we should not take part in no wars, no way, fashion or form, which take the lives of other humans, unless it's a holy war declared by God himself.

MICHAEL: But if it ever came to a war between black and white, you would fight then?

ALI: It would have to be a holy war declared by God himself. Some black man go out and start something, a riot, I'm not gonna jump in it and get killed, or if I don't believe in what he's fighting for, or I don't agree with his approach.

'I'm not just a boxer. I do a lot of studying, a lot of reading.'

MICHAEL: You see your own place very clearly as an athlete and as a figure in this particular dispute we've been talking about – what about other black athletes, like say Patterson as an example, Floyd Patterson.

ALI: Oh he's completely the opposite of me, he ain't no way like me.

MICHAEL: Precisely, that's why I'm asking you about him. What do you think about the other black athletes like him who in their time have had influence, or would have been in a position to have influenced people, about their attitude, which is certainly slightly more moderate than yours?

ALI: Well, they go down in history as just being an athlete. I'm given more praise and credit for what I'm doing now on this show than for coming here and beating five of your English champions. Right now black people are jumping, shouting, because they don't have the nerve to say what I'm saying and nobody's never said it and they're just so happy to see a black man who will stand up and jeopardise every quarter he's got to tell the truth. So like Floyd Patterson and other fighters, they just don't take part. They make a million dollars, they get them a Rolls-Royce, they get them a nice home, they get them a white wife – he won't say nothing. But when one man of popularity can let the world know the problem – he might lose a few dollars telling the truth, but he's helping millions. I just love the freedom and the flesh and blood of my people more so than I do the money. You couldn't get Joe Frazier, no boxer on this show, and get an interesting subject like this.

MICHAEL: That's true. You mentioned earlier on about the fear that you have, and every fighter must have, of getting his face messed up.

ALI: No, I don't really fear that, cos I control it. See, I don't control the airplane or the pilot or what he's doing. So when I'm in the ring I'm handling it and I don't worry about nobody being that good to really hurt me, see?

MICHAEL: What about the other thing that could happen in boxing, the brain damage?

ALI: I look at other fighters fighting, I say I must be a fool. Here are two men, like two roosters, and the roosters are fighting each other and they're not even mad, don't know each other, but just to please somebody. And here are two men in the ring fighting each other and they're hitting each other, and they bleed and they're fighting – what they mad about? They're not mad about nothing, just a bunch of agitating bloodthirsty people saying my man can whoop your man. Human beings, it's real savage. And I said, I'm not gonna be that kind of fighter, I want to dance and be pretty. I'm just gonna win on points. If I hurt my man I'm gonna let him go, I'm not gonna kill him just because somebody's watching.

MICHAEL: What plans do you have for the future now, apart from fighting?

'I am the greatest. I am beautiful. If you talk jive you'll fall in five!'

ALI: Well, I'll tell you something. I don't think I've ever said this before but I'll tell you. I really care nothing about boxing. Boxing is a stepping stone just to introduce me to the audience. Like if I was still in Louisville, Kentucky, and never was a boxer, I might get killed next week in some type of freedom struggle and you'd never read the news. But now if I even say the wrong thing it makes the news. So boxing is just to introduce me to the struggle, like when I speak I draw people in the States, I draw my people to teach and various things, which have given dignity and pride . . . We have the dope and prostitution problem, and I use my image to help. I do all I can to stop a lot of trouble going on with people fighting and killing each other. So boxing is just going to be another year. My main fight is for freedom and equality, and this is what I plan to do and boxing is good for a livelihood. Even today, if my title hadn't been given back to me, if I'd got into such poverty that I had to go find out a job, I would have did that. But I make a good living speaking in colleges, cos the war got unpopular and I was naturally right in the middle of all of it, represented it . . . So number one comes freedom first of my people, and equality, and this is what I plan to do after I'm through fighting – working with nothing but the people, little people, in the alleys, the wine-heads, the downtrodden people, going out among them and helping them with my image.

MICHAEL: Can I ask you before we have to close down—

ALI: One hour's gone by already?

MICHAEL: Yeah, already.

ALI: Oh, time flies when you're in good company, don't it?

MICHAEL: There's talk about a rematch with Frazier, and anybody who saw the first fight I'm sure would be – that's what they want to see, because it was a great fight, it's one of the best fights I've ever seen, I think. Are you gonna make a prediction about your return?

ALI: Well I have a poem. Can I have one minute? The poem goes like this:

People say what's gonna happen, when you gonna meet Joe Frazier again, this is how the fight's gonna sound on the radio for those who can't afford to buy the expensive theatre seats. And the fight goes like this:

Ding, Ali comes out to meet Frazier but Frazier starts
   to retreat,
If Frazier goes back any further he'll wind up in a
   ringside seat,
Ali swings to the left, Ali swings to the right, look at
   the kid carry the fight,
Frazier keeps backing, but there's not enough room,
It's a matter of time, then Ali lowers the boom,
Now Ali lands to the right – what a beautiful swing,
And deposits Frazier clean out of the ring.
Frazier's still rising, but the referee wears a frown

For he can't start counting till Frazier comes down.

Now Frazier disappears from view, the crowd is getting
    frantic,

But our radar stations have picked him up,

He's somewhere over the Atlantic.

Who would of thought when they came to the fight,

That they would have witnessed the launching of a
    coloured satellite!

MICHAEL: Muhammad Ali, thanks a lot.

ALI: I have one more poem about your show – two seconds.
I asked how much money was I getting, you know, for
taking up all my time, you know. I used to get a little pay
for this. And they said your budget's kind of low and you
don't pay too much. So I wrote a poem and I'm gonna
close with this:

I love your show, and I like your style,

But your pay is so cheap I won't be back for a while!

Chapter 3

THE ROAD TO THE SECOND PARKINSON INTERVIEW

1972–1974

Ken Norton, former Marine – in any other era of boxing he would have been the best around.

Chapter 3

'Boxing owes Muhammad Ali a lot more than he owes boxing.'

Ken Norton, American former heavyweight boxer

ALI was now in the unfamiliar position of being the underdog. No longer first in the queue to fight for the championship, he had to work his way back to the top of the list, and it would be another three years before the king in exile regained his crown. And like all kings in exile, he established his own court to underline his superiority to the present incumbent. To be a constant reminder that, one day, he would return to claim what was rightfully his. His court was situated at Deer Lake, Pennsylvania. It had a dining hall, a fully equipped gym, bungalows for sparring partners and guests. It was where Ali would train for the rest of his career, and it was also where this 'king across the water' gathered his entourage around him, with Dundee as his High Chamberlain and long-term friend and fixer Bundini Brown as his court jester.

Everything was focused on the return bout with Frazier, but then in January 1973 Smokin' Joe was battered by a twenty-five-year-old George Foreman in Kingston, Jamaica, and now there were two dragons to slay. Frazier for redemption and Foreman for the crown.

For most of Ali's career, his opponents were chosen with great care. Apart from the big three of Liston, Frazier and Foreman, they were generally fighters who were past their peak. Now, at this critical juncture in Ali's career, Dundee and Herbert Muhammad, his manager, made a big mistake: they matched him with former Marine, Ken Norton. It was, however, a mistake that would reveal the full depth of Ali's desire and courage.

In the second round of the fight, Norton broke Ali's jaw so badly that he would have to have a ninety-minute operation to reconstruct the jaw. Yet Ali fought on for a further ten rounds, losing on points.

Ferdie Pacheco was amazed by his courage on that night. 'He's an incredible gritty son of a bitch. The pain must have been awful. He couldn't fight his fight because he had to protect his jaw. And still, he fought the whole twelve rounds. God Almighty, was that guy tough . . . underneath all that beauty, there was an ugly Teamsters Union Trucker at work.'

It is, to the average person, unimaginable the level of mental toughness and physical courage required to endure the kind of physical hell Ali put himself through in those remaining rounds. What drove him on was the fact that, for his career, it was a fight he couldn't lose, and the fact that every fight Ali took part in was more than just a fight. He was the standard-bearer for the black Muslims, a holy warrior in the cause of black civil rights in a country that had just elected Richard Nixon and was still engaged in the Vietnam War.

But lose he did, and for many this spelled the end for Ali. He was thirty-one, over the hill, good only as a punchbag for up-and-coming fighters. But he was far from finished. In fact the most glorious, golden period of his career was in front of him.

Six months after having his jaw rewired, on 10 September 1973, he stepped back into the ring with Ken Norton, and although even on points entering the twelfth and final round, Ali pulled out all the stops and won a unanimous decision.

Frazier was again in his sights, but not before the verbal war stepped up in intensity. Ali called Frazier ignorant; Frazier called him Clay. It got to the stage where they couldn't be in the same room, even if they were on TV.

Chapter 4

ROUND 2, PARKINSON/DICK CAVETT, ABC/BBC CO-PRODUCTION, ABC STUDIOS, NEW YORK CITY

25 January 1974

Punchin' Parky.

'Some people can see further than others ...'

Henry's Hammer gives the British public hope, 18 June 1963.

'Like being in the ring with a bleeding tank.' Our 'enry after the fight.

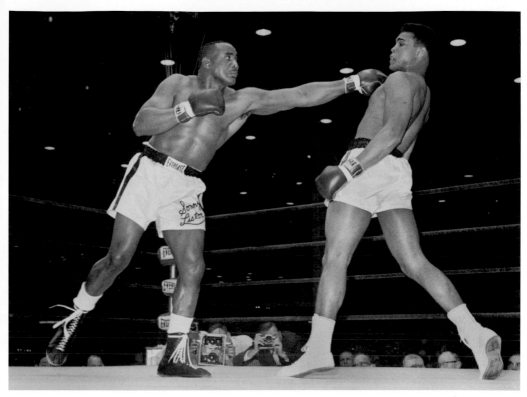

Hunting the Big Ugly Bear. Ali v. Liston 1, world heavyweight championship fight, 25 February 1964.

Ali v. Liston 2, 25 May 1965. 'Get up and fight, sucker!' Ali knocks Liston out in the first round.

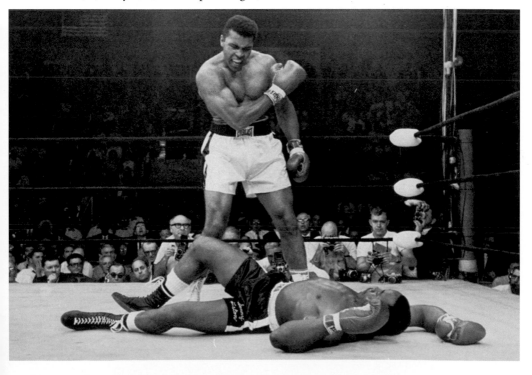

Ali v. Frazier, Superfight 1, 8 March 1971. The comeback stalls.

'What's my name?' Ali reminds Ernie Terrell of his proper name whilst rearranging his features, 6 February 1967.

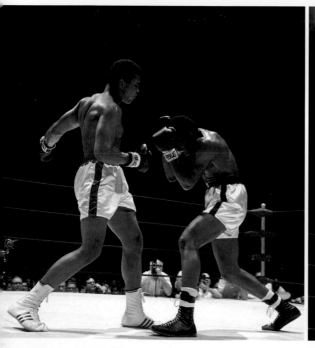

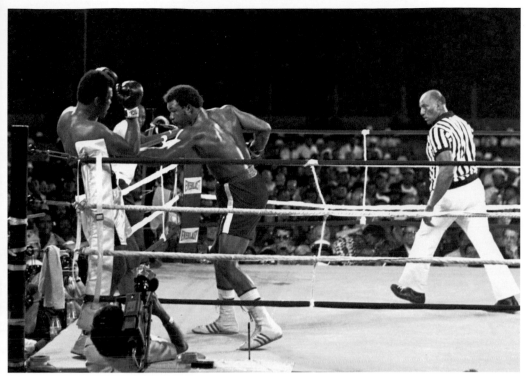

'Come on, show me something, show me something, kid, you're not doing nothing, you're just a girl, look at you!' The Rumble in the Jungle, 30 October 1974. Ali rope-a-dopes while goading Foreman.

'This is the wrong place to get tired.' Ali knocks out Foreman in the eighth round to reclaim the heavyweight title, 30 October 1974.

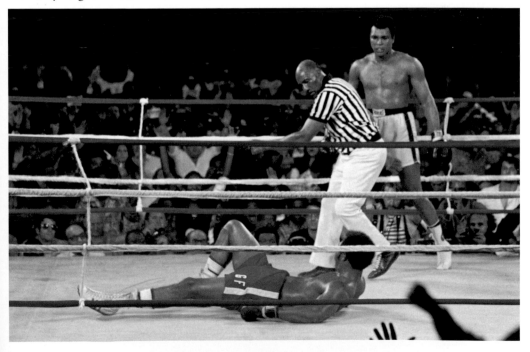

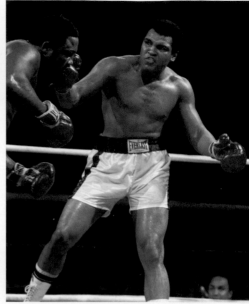

Ali v. Frazier, Superfight 3, 1 October 1975. A terrifying, brutal assault over fourteen rounds by both men.

Frazier: the fighter that defined Ali as a boxer. The one he couldn't dominate, the itch he couldn't scratch.

'The closest thing to dying.' With Ali close to collapse, Frazier remains on his stool at the end of the fourteenth. Neither would be the same fighter after this bout, 1 October 1975.

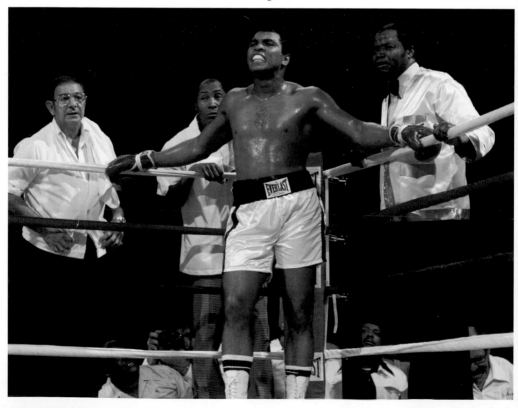

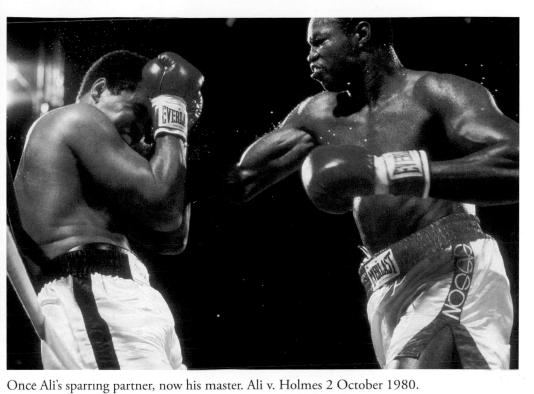

Once Ali's sparring partner, now his master. Ali v. Holmes 2 October 1980.

Ali staring defeat and humiliation in the face. Ali v. Holmes, 2 October 1980.

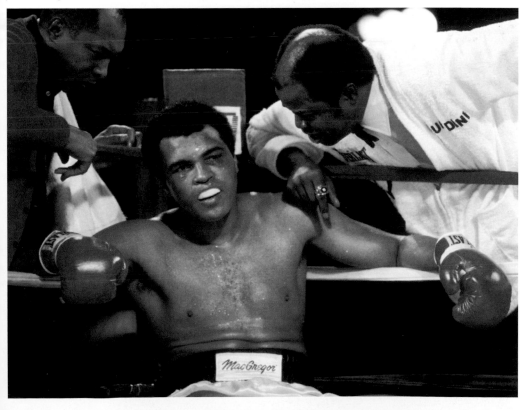

Left: At the premiere of the film *Ali,* with an awe-struck Will Smith and son.

Below: Dignified and brave, lighting the Olympic torch at the Salt Lake City Games in 2002.

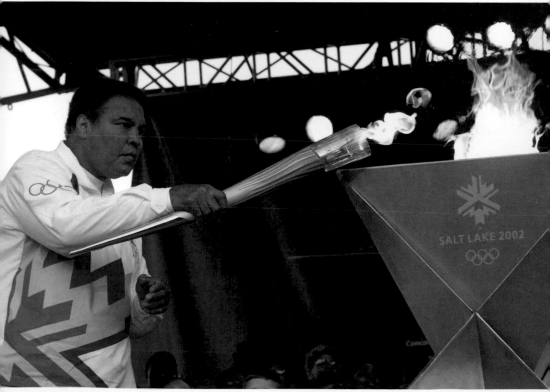

Chapter 4

'Fifteen referees. I want fifteen referees to be at this fight, because there ain't no one man who can keep up with the pace I'm gonna set.'

Muhammad Ali

MUHAMMAD Ali did wonders for the *Parkinson* show. Indeed, across the years we could guarantee a substantial increase in viewing figures whenever he appeared. The British audience loved him. Even his extreme views on black and white seemed to amuse rather than enrage. One day, Richard Drewett, my producer, read that a return match with Frazier was being planned and thought it might be a good idea to take the show to New York, to persuade Ali and Frazier to appear together and transmit the show via satellite back to England. We were encouraged in our enthusiasm by participating in the first transatlantic talk show when I had Jackie Stewart and Jonathan Miller in London talking to Mort Sahl and Bette Davis in New York. This was a joint production with Dick Cavett's

American production company. The technology was far from perfect. The delay on projecting sound across the Atlantic meant a delay of four or five seconds, making a flowing conversation impossible. In fact, Jonathan Miller worked out if he died in London he would have a few seconds more in America before they heard the death rattle.

The BBC said it was enthusiastic, but thought the cost might be a problem, so could we find a co-production deal? We approached Dick Cavett, who jumped at the idea, and so off we went to New York.

Richard and I booked in for a week's preparation before the event. That was when I began to have misgivings about Cavett. I felt he wanted to take over the show, to make it appear not so much a joint production, more a Dick Cavett event, with the country cousin from England making a fleeting appearance. We relied on Cavett's organisation for our basic research because, in those days before the Internet, access to research was a tedious and time-consuming business. Moreover, we needed to get together with Cavett and his production team to plot the interview, to work out who talked to whom and when.

With a couple of days to go, and having been continually stalled by the Cavett office, we were finally convinced that the so-called collaboration had, in fact, become a contest. What we were experiencing, of course, was the ultra-competitive cut-throat business of American television. By contrast, British television was a benign industry, mollycoddled by the knowledge that any share of a three-channel market was substantial enough to keep everyone happy.

I phoned Mr Cavett and asked him how we would manage dividing the interview. He said he thought we might 'wing it'. I said we had both been in the business long enough to know that 'winging it' was not the way to make a successful show. We left it at that.

On the day of the recording I was angry and disgruntled at the prospect of doing a show that had been our idea but which had been effectively hijacked. I was made to feel even further from home when, while sitting in make-up, I was approached by one of Cavett's staff who said, 'Dick wanted you to have this.' He handed me a document which contained a plan of how the show would go and included smart replies and gags to the responses his questions might provoke.

What I didn't know, but came to realise, was that Dick Cavett and Muhammad Ali were close and the fighter was a regular on the show. When he died I read that Ali had been on the Cavett show fourteen or fifteen times and the two men were firm friends. Foolishly, perhaps, I had thought the show might be a good chance to explore the feelings and ambitions of two boxers who were about to inflict serious and potentially lasting damage on each other. Cavett saw it as a chance to promote a car crash in the studio between two men who couldn't wait to pummel each other into a hospital bed. And that is what happened.

Ali produced the full lexicon of abuse for Frazier, who struggled to return fire and mostly sat in grim-visaged anger until Ali provoked him into removing his jacket and squaring up in the studio. It was then we saw Ali the vaudevillian at his best. His soft-shoe shuffle as the two men faced each other, fists raised, was perfect in its timing and comic effect. Chaplin would have been proud of it.

Ali also revealed another, more sensitive side of his nature. The longer the show lasted, the more it became obvious I was surplus to requirements. It was my fault. I had been either unable or unwilling to join in the circus. I felt like an uninvited guest at an orgy. I was paralysed with ineptitude. Ali caught my mood. During a commercial break, he turned to me and said, 'What are you doing here, man?' I said I was sulking, unable to get a word in.

Coming back from the commercial break, Ali announced to our host that he wasn't going to bother answering his questions for a while because he was going to speak to his friend from London, who was not only a better interviewer than Mr Cavett, but also much better looking. That let me in. It was a generous gesture, which contrasted vividly with his cruel taunting of Frazier.

I had grown to admire Joe Frazier. In the run-up to our interview I visited his training camp in Philadelphia and persuaded him to let me spar with him as an overture to the TV show. Philadelphia became Frazier's home once he left South Carolina. Angelo Dundee, Ali's trainer, once said, 'Philadelphia is not a town. It's a jungle. They don't have gyms here, they have zoos. They don't have sparring sessions, they have wars.'

I have never felt as alien as I did when I entered the ring in Frazier's gym. I was kitted out in shorts and a white T-shirt with 'Smokin' Joe' across the front. The wiseguys at ringside who had come to see Frazier work out regarded me with amused contempt. Joe was charming and solicitous. He didn't even laugh when we stripped and changed in the same dressing room. All that can be said about a comparison between our two physiques is that not only was God very clever, but He also had a wonderful sense of humour.

My borrowed shorts had obviously belonged to a Sumo wrestler. My arms, which have always been on the skinny side, looked even more puny with boxing gloves the size of pillow cases attached to the ends.

As I clambered into the ring, I felt the curiosity of the audience turn to hate. These were true boxing aficionados, men who frequent gymnasiums and watch boxers work out, men who had faces as battered as a blind cobbler's thumb.

They gave me a glance, shook their heads, and no doubt thought the champ was soft in the head to get mixed up in a publicity stunt with a famine victim. When we shook hands, it suddenly struck me that Frazier's arms were the size of my legs and the circumference of his neck nearly matched that of my chest.

Beforehand, in the dressing room, the former heavyweight champion of the world had asked me about my previous experience. I told him I had fought Sonny Shaw in the playground at the Snydale Road Infants' School, Cudworth, and a Lance Corporal Smithers in an army barracks at Devizes. Frazier said he didn't know either fighter, but all I had to do for the purpose of our encounter was to keep on jabbing, whereupon he would move inside, pretend to throw a few punches, and whisper the next move in my ear.

He was as good as his word, and better. He would slip inside my tentative left arm, hammer away at my body as if he meant it, but all the time just pulling the punch an inch from the point of contact. Then he would spin me round like a dancing partner, whisper 'left hook, right hook' and move away.

Soon my fear deserted me. Soon, I began to believe it was Smokin' Joe versus Punchin' Parky. It was a dangerous illusion. Joe was choreographing the third and final round and making it look believable when I decided to change the script.

As Joe came in, slipping my lead, I swung a right which hit him on the side of the head. As I did it I realised my mistake. After all, I had struck a man who had been the heavyweight champion of the world, a man who could knock my head off if he so desired. Frazier shook his head in mock confusion, gave me a knowing smile and then hit me with a left hook.

By his definition it was a tap to the head, a gentle

reminder not to be silly. The problem is that fit and strong men like Joe Frazier have little idea of their own strength in relation to the rest of the human race. He felt he had gently chastised me; I felt as if I had walked into a cement mixer. The legs went at the knees and I heard bells. Frazier raised my hand and walked me round the ring as the victor. In fact he was holding me up.

The spectators kept their eyes firmly on the racing pages and I slumped on a bench, where I was left to contemplate my foolishness as Frazier went to work on the heavy bag. Eddie Futch, his trainer, worked him hard, whipping him to a controlled frenzy by telling him he was punching like a girl, taunting him with the latest Ali prediction until the heavy bag, with the trainer clinging to it, was being moved from side to side and backwards and forwards by the ferocity of the blows.

When Futch wrapped it up with, 'OK champ, that's enough for the day,' Frazier turned from the bag, sweat pouring from him, eyes glinting with anger. He was looking for something to hit. He drove his fist into the pine strip wall of the gymnasium with such power that it dislodged an air-conditioning unit.

A few days later, we sat together in a television studio

while Muhammad Ali took over the show, as he always did when given an even chance.

It was one of Ali's more extraordinary performances. He wasn't selling tickets. He didn't need to. He was involving us all in his fantasies, demonstrating the full range of his remarkable personality. One moment he would be sensibly reflecting upon the reasons why he chose not to be drafted in the American Army, and the next he would be taunting Joe Frazier to the limit, calling him 'dumb', asking how he thought he had the right to share a stage with one so clever and pretty, timing the insult so perfectly that, as Frazier rose from his seat, excited and angry, to confront his tormentor, we were back on air and Ali was revealed having a joke with the hosts, while Frazier, for no reason the viewers could discern, was on his feet looking grim and menacing, his fists at the ready.

The studio confrontation we devised was certainly an event but little else. All we had learned was what we already knew, that each man intensely disliked the other. Nor had the show done anything to cement Anglo-American television relations, Mr Cavett being swept away in a limo before I had the chance of a word in his ear.

Edited transcript of interview

MICHAEL: What's the point of insulting each other, though? I mean you insult everybody before a fight.

ALI: The Garden is sold out. That's why. I thought you, I thought you had more intelligence. This is a big man in London. Like Johnny Carson, he ain't no big thing in London, Dick Cavett ain't nothing in London. So look, in London this is the Johnny Carson. Everybody know him. I was on his show once. How many times did you run that show it was so good?

MICHAEL: Four or five times.

ALI: Four or five times. We were debating on religion, race, drought, boxing, on everything. They ran that show four or five times.

MICHAEL: What happens if you lose?

ALI: What happens if I lose?

DICK: Good question.

ALI: I can't lose. I'm not worried about losing. I really don't think about it. I've never made preparations for loss. I'm moving like I should move. I'm no longer playing. I'm boxing. This man comes in and anybody can hit him, all his sparring partners are ramming him every day. And there's nothing to me, no class, no footwork, no speed, when I get those itty-bitty gloves on and be real serious and no playing, no staying in the corner.

FRAZIER: Wonder what they're going to put on me . . . What kind of gloves I'm going to have?

ALI: I'll prove, he can't stop me. Nobody stops me.

FRAZIER: What kind of gloves am I going to have on? You answer that . . . What kind of gloves am I going to have on?

ALI: You'll have the same gloves you have on last time. The same things you had last time.

FRAZIER: You gonna have little gloves? What they gonna put on me? Sledgehammer or something?

ALI: That sounds silly, another crazy question. Everybody knows he's going to have on gloves like me.

FRAZIER: All right, but why are you making a statement like that?

ALI: What am I going to have on? OK. You going to have on gloves like me. And we always have on the same, let's just get going now. [Ali & Frazier stand up to fight]

FRAZIER: Any time. Any time.

ALI: Don't back out. Put your coat down, don't back out.

DICK: You could hit him accidentally and break a finger or something.

ALI: I could hit him accidentally. What do you think I'm trying to do?

DICK: Why, anything you like.

FRAZIER: He's trying to hit me.

ALI: Oh, I can't wait. I can't wait.

Ali selling tickets; Frazier playing it for real – New York, 25 January 1974.

FRAZIER: Oh, I want you so bad.

DICK: You'd better sit down.

ALI: You want me so bad?

FRAZIER: So bad. I just can't wait.

ALI: Boy, you gonna be in trouble.

DICK: I'd love to see you fight, but your trainer just fainted because he knows you can hurt a finger this way or something and the fight would be over . . . What if a twelve-year-old kid came to you? A twelve-year-old black kid or white kid, either one. Listen, listen, and he said, 'I got a good physique and I want to fight. I'm twelve years old.' Would you tell him to go into professional boxing?

ALI: Number one, I say kid, your chances of being a great, good enough to make a good living is about a hundred thousand to one. And if you spend the most of your life trying to be a fighter and you get hurt or you don't make it, your whole life is ruined. It's too late to get education. It's too late to look for trade or something to fall back on. I say no. Take your education. Train your mind while you're quick for developing, learn to read, learn to write, be a mechanic, be a doctor, be a lawyer. Go now, learn, get your mind conditioned. You can't be like Muhammad Ali or Joe Frazier. We are two little black boys, who came up to be the biggest draws in the whole world. And don't think cos I made it, I'm going to tell you to box, no. Get your brains together, box for exercise, but get your brains together, get educated and get a trade; because you might not make it, there's too much risk involved. No, go to school. That's the best thing. That's the best thing to tell him.

MICHAEL: How can you justify boxing as a sport? To those people who say it's not a sport. That it's hateful.

ALI: Hateful?

MICHAEL: Yep. Immoral.

ALI: Well it's the action, it's the action. I'll tell you this. It's immoral number one when the blacks are dominating.

113

Beginning to wonder what I'm doing here.

MICHAEL: Oh that's nonsense.

ALI: No, let me tell you. I'm telling you.

MICHAEL: That argument's as old as boxing itself.

ALI: Let me tell you. It's the action. It's the purpose that makes the thing right or wrong. The same judge can say I'm right for killing him, but wrong for killing you. Why'd I kill him? I caught him molesting my wife. I don't get a day in jail. I kill you over who's gonna win this fight, both of the actions was killing, but what determines them right or wrong is the purpose. Our purpose is not to kill one another in the ring. Our purpose is not to kill – it's not immoral as long as our purpose is not immoral.

MICHAEL: But what, what, what kind of sport is it? Can it be?

ALI: What kind of sport?

MICHAEL: When a guy goes in a ring, gets his jaw broken.

ALI: What kind of sport is this? When a guy gets into a damn car in your country and go round a damn track and hit a pole and he burn up. What kind of sport is that? And a bunch of fools who are watching . . . Don't get on our little sport. We don't have nothing or no way for a job, few of us can't get nothing, unless we can box, and now you want to run that out. Well you go over to England and stop some of your sports. I don't see any black folks out there going nine hundred million miles [Ali makes a car noise and explosion]. You get on them, don't get on us.

In many ways the fight was like the interview, the anticipation being of a higher order than the actual result. The fight was something of an anti-climax. It was bound to be so when compared to the first encounter. Frazier lost, but only just, and Ali went on to regain the title and dream anew. Before and after the fight I sent these reports to *The Sunday Times* in London.

The Overture

The worst part is over. The insults and the scuffling on television are finished, the hullabaloo is muted and the publicity men can reflect proudly on their part in a campaign which had as its intellectual highlight a mock fight between Muhammad Ali and a dwarf, run close by the spectacle of two of the world's greatest athletes rolling around the floor of a television studio like common street fighters.

Herbie, the world's worst waiter, and himself an expert in the art of mediocrity, is of the opinion that everything so far has been 'crap'. We should respect Herbie's opinion because he is so bad at his job he has become an institution, and the management at Costello's, where he works, have threatened to sack him if he shows any signs of improvement. He treads his beat between the tables, spilling gravy, sticking his fingers in the soup, leaving his thumb print in the butter. A monument to man's ability to misuse that miracle of design, the human body.

Costello's is a watering hole frequented by journalists and sundry wordsmiths in New York. It is a place used to excessive and outrageous behaviour and, therefore, as good a place as any to judge what has happened so far and what might happen tomorrow.

The first thing to be said is, in the words of the immortal Herbie: 'There ain't no way this night will be what it used to be once.' Which is to say that although a sell-out, although billed as a Superfight II, there is nothing like the atmosphere and tension that surrounded the first fight. Which is no bad thing since that event was the most pretentiously oversold product of all time. Some claimed it as a religious contest, crescent against cross; others said it was a political fight with Mr OK taking on the draft-dodger; while others of a more romantic frame of mind visualised it as a collision of opposites, poet versus peasant.

In fact, what happened was that two superbly trained and splendidly fit heavyweight prizefighters did their best to inflict maximum hurt on each other for fifteen rounds, and stuck to their task so well that they both ended up in hospital.

With any amount of luck the same thing is likely to happen in Madison Square Garden in spite of the fact that both men have had three years in which to remember the damage they caused each other, that this time there is no title to be fought for and, moreover, in spite of a rise in the cost of living, both men are taking a cut in salary.

Perhaps the simple truth of the matter is the one uttered by Ali after the last fight when asked what he thought of Frazier now. 'He's just another brother earning a living,' he said.

He has said nothing as revealing, truthful or generous these past few days. What we have seen is the old, but everlastingly entertaining routine of belittling his opponent, chopping him down with the rapid fire of his insult and mockery. As usual he has come up against little opposition, Frazier being at first unwilling and finally unable to trade invective.

There is nothing edifying in watching one man, blessed with a quick mind and a forked tongue, abusing another who, by comparison, appears illiterate. Neither is the spectacle improved by it taking place on stage where Ali struts and dominates like the born actor he is and Frazier flounders helplessly like some beached sea monster. All that saves Ali on occasions like those we have witnessed in the past few days is his own instinct for turning potential tragedy into broad farce and the certain knowledge that, in spite of all he says, he is incapable of hating anyone or anything.

If there be a virtue in watching Ali flush his opponent down the pan it is that he demonstrates to all of us the worst aspects of boxing. He aims his jibes at Frazier, but, in fact, he is taunting all of us, challenging our real values, daring us to deny that what we want to see is hatred and fury and controlled violence.

'All you nice respectable people payin' lots of money to see two black boys whuppin' each other. You ought to be ashamed of yourselves,' he said the other day, shortly after humiliating Frazier in front of the television cameras. Two minutes before, during a commercial break, he had removed his coat and started dancing in front of Frazier, flicking out his left hand, missing Frazier's chin by inches. Then his eyes started rolling, beads of sweat appeared on his face and his voice became high and excitable. He seemed to be out of control. Frazier looked wary and rose from his seat to defend himself. The floor manager started counting us back into the programme. With five seconds to go Ali stopped as suddenly as he had started and sat in his chair, perfectly composed, like a man who has just had a refreshing cat nap. He looked at the rest of us, who were excited and aroused and gave us a smile both knowing and scornful.

Frazier's discomfort on these occasions is painful to see and there can be little doubt that, whereas Ali's attitudes are calculated and phoney, Frazier's hatred of his opponent is a very real and potentially deadly thing.

He cannot express it adequately in words and, therefore, I sense he stores it, a reservoir of loathing timed to overflow on the night. At the pre-fight medical – another Ali-inspired comic opera – it was Frazier who had the last chilling words. 'When that bell goes he's going to be in front of me, and that's for sure,' he said. 'And that's all I want,' he added.

It lacked the tinsel glitter of Ali's performance a few moments before, but it was twice as effective. For twenty minutes Ali had run through his entire repertoire ranging from fool to sage. 'He has too many lumps; so he must fall on his rump,' he rhymed, but only just. He then went into a slapstick cross-talk routine with fellow-jester Drew Bundini, an extract of which will give you some idea of the quality:

Ali: 'Are we goin' to dance?'

Bundini: 'All night long.'

'Are we going to beat his head?'

'He knows it.'

'Joe Frazier has no future.'

'He knows that too.'

'I am going to do something unusual to dat man.'

'He'd better believe it.'

Both fighters were delighted to know that they had passed the medical. Ali's right hand, which he had been nursing, was declared perfect. 'Ah know'd it all along. I was just makin' a big technicolour production number for the world to worry about,' he said. The only thing wrong with Frazier, said the doctor, was that he needed a shave.

All very reassuring and dispelling any doubts that we might be watching a couple of stumble-bums in action. And yet there are lingering doubts about both men. An x-ray machine can tell you many things, but not the state of a man's mind. Both men have had the time to contemplate the future, to brood on the pain and the dangers of their profession. Both are in a situation where they can only view the future by looking downward and not skyward.

If they are motivated by anything this time round it is pride. Ali has a score to settle, a world to please. Frazier, battered by Ali's words, wants the big man in a situation where he has to do his talking with his fists. Moreover he has to re-establish his own pride in his craft after so obviously abusing it in his fight with Foreman.

This time they meet without all the intellectual baloney that threatened to turn their last fight into a debate on the meaning of life. This time the scenario is simple: two old gunslingers come to town looking for each other. This is the final showdown and for one of them there is no way back. For the other there is little future, simply the prospect of a dignified retirement. It might not be colourful enough for Muhammad Ali, but that is the way it is.

The Aftermath, 1974

The greatest athletes are those who play to their own rules and triumph according to their own star. They operate at the highest aesthetic level, blending athletic skill, grace and intelligence into a moving and irresistible spectacle.

To many people, myself included, the boxing ring is not the place where such a spectacle is to be found. Of course we see skill, and grace and intelligence and courage, but, in the end, they must be balanced against the brutality of the sport, the fact that boxing's basic premise is for one man to knock another senseless.

It took a special man to persuade me otherwise and it is a mark of his genius that Muhammad Ali did so – for me and a billion others besides. His gift was that he had something for everyone. His skills satisfied even the most critical boxing buff, when it came to ballyhoo he made Barnum and Bailey look like non-starters, and he had the incandescent quality of the real star which would have made him world-famous even if his gift was knitting and not fighting.

More than any other athlete he involved the world in his fantasies, wove us all into the pattern of his dreams. He made predictions which failed and we pretended we hadn't heard them, he bellowed at the moon and we nodded our approval, and his most spectacular achievement was that he turned his defeats into victories and we believed him.

In the end he tried the impossible: he endeavoured to defy time and the passing years and at Madison Square Garden in January 1974 we saw that not even he can do that. All right, he won, and there are those who were there, whose opinions I respect, who say it was a great fight and that he won marvellously, a victory to herald the second coming. In contrast I saw a man win not because of his genius, but because of workmanlike application and the accumulated knowledge of the old pro.

There were moments of the former magic, particularly at the very beginning and towards the end of the fight, but in spite of what he says he can no longer 'float like a butterfly and sting like a bee'. Too often he gained respite and neutralised Frazier by the simple and illegal expedient of placing his left glove behind Frazier's neck and pulling him close and off balance.

Referee Perez, nervous and frail as a grasshopper, would yell 'break', but nothing happened. He'd repeat the order and still Ali smothered Frazier, buying time. Later Frazier and his trainer Eddie Futch were quick to criticise the referee for allowing Ali's tactics. Futch said, 'Clay did it to Ken Norton in both fights – I know because I worked Norton's corner. Before the fight I asked Perez about it and he said he'd see to it. I talked to him again after the fifth, but he did nothing. Clay does it all the time now because he's slowed down and cannot put that much fighting into each round.'

In contrast to Ali's often negative behaviour there was something noble and admirable in Frazier's blind determination to make a fight of it. He epitomises the honest slugger, the man who leads with his head and takes four shots to get one in. The nature of his style has inevitably meant a dulling of his ability and all the fight proved was that Frazier had deteriorated more rapidly than Ali. The courage was undimmed, but nowadays there is more sound than fury in his punching and one can only hope that he takes the hint and retires on his considerable earnings.

During the build-up I learned to like and admire Frazier a lot and it would be tragic if he continued to take further beatings in vain pursuit of the title. It would be equally tragic if he settled for some quick money fighting the lesser fry.

As for Ali he is still embarked on his dream and is still good enough to mess with the best of them. He knows sufficient to give the untutored Foreman a lot of trouble, but the outcome of their fight must inevitably depend on its timing. In terms of passing years Foreman can afford to wait. Ali cannot. Not that he would ever admit it.

After the fight he sat sucking an iced lolly, surrounded by his court. 'If I'd have got whupped you'd have wrote I was finished. Do I look whupped, do I look old, is there a mark on the face?' Someone suggested his nose was bleeding. Ali withered him with a glance. 'Nose bleed,' he said scornfully. 'Ah'm talking about real marks, cuts and bruises, now tell me do you see any?' There weren't any. The face was as unmarked and fresh as a choirboy's.

He ended the conference with a poem. He told us all to be quiet, settle back, looked at the ceiling, paused for dramatic effect and then said something like 'Truth, the face of truth is open.' The rest was lost in his delivery which tends at times to speed ahead of his thoughts and certainly ahead of most journalists' shorthand.

But he had raised an interesting subject. What is the truth about Muhammad Ali? What we saw in Madison Square Garden was both a decline and a change, and the two are related. The poet outside the ring is no longer the poet inside it. The greatest artist and entertainer in the history of the game is nowadays a professional and canny prizefighter. There is nothing wrong in that, in merely being one of the best fighters in the game, except if you happen to be Muhammad Ali.

Chapter 5

THE ROAD TO THE THIRD PARKINSON INTERVIEW
January 1974—December 1974

'Now you must meet me, your master!' Foreman v. Ali, 30 October 1974.

Chapter 5

'Joe Frazier is too ugly to be champ. Joe Frazier is too dumb to be champ. The heavyweight champion should be smart and pretty like me.'

Muhammad Ali

ALI's victory over Frazier in January 1974 settled nothing between them. Ali couldn't dominate Frazier, couldn't stop him raining down hurtful, damaging punches on his head and to the body. Ali only won by using superior ring craft, mixing holding with brief moments of accurate flurry-punching to impress the judges. This inability to produce a defining victory over Frazier was, I believe, at the core of Ali's hatred of the man. Frazier frightened Ali as a fighter in a way that no one else had ever or would ever do. He was the one chink in his armour of invincibility, the itch he couldn't scratch, and that would anger and frustrate a man as proud and vainglorious as Ali.

This unconvincing victory ensured there would be another

rematch, but not before he truly took on the mantle of greatness by defeating the monstrous George Foreman on a stormy October night in Zaire.

All change at the top. Foreman destroys Frazier to take the world heavyweight crown, 22 January 1973.

Foreman, like Liston before him, was considered unbeatable. He had destroyed Norton and Frazier, fighters who had caused Ali both difficulties and damage. Furthermore, unlike the Liston fight, Ali didn't have youth on his side. Foreman was twenty-five, Ali was thirty-one. No one, not even his personal court, gave him a chance. But Ali knew better. He had his innate sense of destiny and the full support of the Nation of Zaire.

Zaire's President Mobutu was willing to part with $10 million to stage the fight to show that his country, formerly the centre of the world's ivory and slave trade, epitomised by Joseph Conrad as the heart of darkness had thrown off its imperialist shackles and was a modern, ambitious, capable nation.

As one poster read on the highway from the airport: 'A fight between two blacks in a Black Nation, organised by Blacks and seen by the whole world. That was a victory for Mobutism.'

But not a victory for common sense or decency. It was a fight where two black men would earn $5 million each in a country run by a kleptocratic dictator in a continent ravaged by poverty and famine.

Not that any of this concerned Ali. He was revelling

in being in a country run and operated by black men, and basking in the strength of the affection he was held in by Zairians everywhere. King Ali and his travelling court had found his kingdom. But amidst the fun and the usual Ali grandstanding, he knew that if he ever wanted to exorcise the demons of his years in boxing exile, if he ever wanted to justify his segregationist stance on race relations, his sincere belief in the need for black pride and self-determination, this was a fight he could not lose.

At four a.m. on 30 October 1974, 60,000 spectators, and millions watching in theatres on closed-circuit televisions worldwide, held their breath as the referee called the two fighters together.

Foreman stood impassive, cold eyed, a physical embodiment of destructive power. Ali glared back imperiously and said: 'You have heard of me since you were a little boy. Now you must meet me, your master.'

Much has been made of the 'rope-a-dope' tactics that Ali employed. Undeniably the ropes were slacker than usual, but that was more to do with the oppressive heat than a conscious decision on the part of Ali's camp. The plan, as Dundee saw it, was that Ali would avoid getting hit. He would move, stay on his toes, give the straight-punching Foreman different and confusing angles so that, as Foreman tired, Ali would have his chance. Round one went exactly as planned, but Ali discovered that both the weather and the conditioning of Foreman meant he was expending too much energy avoiding being hit. So Ali, to the horror of his ringside team, went to the ropes, employing a strategy that his old trainer Archie Moore had used as he got older. Moore would conserve energy by letting younger fighters throw their shots, blocking them in turn and then attacking when they got tired. This was a real test of skill, endurance and courage against any boxer, but against a puncher like George Foreman it was tantamount to suicide. And yet, for seven rounds Ali leaned against the ropes, inviting Foreman on to him, dancing away when Foreman hit him too hard and all the while talking and goading the man he had nicknamed 'The Mummy'. By the middle of the sixth round, Ali could sense the power ebbing from Foreman and in the eighth he struck. Ten years after he had first won the title he was the champ again. As he drove back to the presidential compound he had used as his training camp, with a violent thunderstorm trumpeting his progression and the roadsides lined with Zairians chanting his name, he felt truly like a king of the world.

Chapter 6

ROUND 3, PARKINSON, THE MAYFAIR HOTEL, LONDON
7 December 1974

An interviewer's dream.

Chapter 6

‛On that night, they'll be waiting everywhere; England, France, Italy, Egypt and Israel will declare a forty-five-minute truce. Saudi Arabia, Iraq, Iran; even Red China and Formosa. Not since time began has there been a night like this.’

Muhammad Ali

THE joy of interviewing Ali was that there was always another miracle to talk about. This time he was celebrating his resurrection. He had beaten George Foreman in what was known as the Rumble in the Jungle and was now world champion. It wasn't simply that he had beaten big old ugly George, but had humiliated him. As the best of our sportswriters, Hugh McIlvanney, observed: ‘We should have known that Muhammad Ali would not settle for any ordinary old resurrection. He had to have an additional flourish. So, having rolled away the rock, he hit George Foreman on the head with it.’

I met Muhammad Ali and his entourage at the Mayfair Theatre where we were to record a one-man show. He was accompanied by a line of bodyguards wearing dark suits and shades. Ali nodded towards them and said, 'This is Brother . . .' and went along the line. I moved forward with hand outstretched. They looked away.

This is how I recalled what followed in my autobiography.

We had decided this would be the interview when we sidestepped the showboating and tried to concentrate on the nature of the man. The problem with interviewing Muhammad Ali was you could never be sure who was going to turn up. This was a man who reinvented himself every morning when he woke up.

What we needed was a quiet studio for a serious one to one; instead we were in a West End theatre crammed with worshipping admirers and an atmosphere ripe for ballyhoo. It all went more or less to plan until I produced a book written by Budd Schulberg, a friend of Ali's. I said it was a fascinating book, pointing out one or two contradictions in his personality made all the more pertinent because Schulberg knew him well.

Ali bridled and said Schulberg was an 'associate' not a friend.

I put to him a quote from the book: 'He [Ali] is devoted to a religious movement that looks on the white race as devils, whose time of deserved destruction is at hand . . . and yet he's got more genuine white friends than any black fighter I have known.' Again, Ali insisted they were not friends but 'associates'. I pushed him further and asked him how he regarded Angelo Dundee, his trainer for many years. He said he was an 'associate'.

He then launched into a diatribe about how whites hated blacks, which included the observation that I was too small mentally and physically to 'trap' him on my TV show, which, in any case, was a joke. This was the first time I had seen Ali become really angry. The eyes were bright with rage. I had witnessed the play-acting when he was fooling around or selling tickets, but this was different.

The audience sensed it, too. This was a side of Ali they hadn't seen before. In America Ali divided the nation; in Britain he was generally admired both as a prizefighter and an amusing talk-show turn. The Ali on stage at the Mayfair Theatre was someone else, angry, racist and confrontational.

I sat listening to his rant, wondering how to deal with it, and decided all I could sensibly do was sit tight until the eruption of anger abated. I tried to analyse what had caused it and came to the conclusion it might have been a fear of being asked to read the offending passage from the Schulberg book, which he would have found a problem because the most extraordinary fact about this remarkable man is that he is semi-literate.

I asked him about his reading difficulties; he said, 'I study life, I study people and I'm educated on this, but when it comes to reading and writing I'm not. I may be illiterate in that but when it comes to common sense . . . I'm rich.'

The interview lurched to an end with both of us sitting back in our seats displaying the kind of body language that left no doubt about what one was thinking of the other. After the show there was no kissy-kissy, you-were-marvellous-darling farewells. He left with his entourage without a goodbye and I remember feeling, regretfully, that it would be unlikely if we met again.

I went to my dressing room where I sat wondering just what had happened and why. I felt I had been clumsy in my approach to the question about his white friends and further concerned that the outburst it had provoked might alienate a part of the audience who had hitherto adored him. My concern was based on the belief I have that, while Ali's faith is genuine, he was exploited as a propaganda outlet by people whose extreme views he might have echoed but never espoused.

I was thinking all these things when there was a knock on my dressing-room door. It was my father, who had been in the audience. As usual he came to the point.

'What do you reckon then?' he asked.

'Not much, Dad,' I said.

'Nor do I.' Then he said, 'Can I ask you a question?'

I nodded.

'What was up with you tonight, our Michael?'

'What do you mean? What on earth could I have done?'

'Why didn't you thump him?' said my father.

I looked at him for a full minute, at the angry determination in his face, and then I started laughing.

Edited transcript of interview

MICHAEL: I think that you win a lot of your fights as well as in the ring, outside the ring. You psych people out, don't you, beforehand?

ALI: You don't want to psych them out, you make them fight harder. You don't psych them out, you don't put fear in them, and that's the thing, it makes them fight too hard, and makes them anxious. They gotta get you, like I told George. I said OK sucker, I'm backing up in the ropes and I want to take your best shots! And I just stood there. Come on, show me something, show me something kid, you're not doing nothing, you're just a girl, look at you! You ain't got nothing! Come on, sucker, show me something, show me something sucker! If you think I'm not telling the truth, watch the films, I talked him to death, and I made him so angry, he just beat hisself out. He was so tired he was swaying and just falling on the ropes. I said, man, this is the wrong place to get tired. It worries the man to beat him and talk to him, you understand?

MICHAEL: Do they talk back to you?

ALI: No. Only one fellow talked back to me and that's Joe Frazier. I hit Joe Frazier with about ninety punches. If you remember the first fight, hit him with everything. The man took a terrible beating, he wouldn't fall. I said, 'Are you crazy?' I said, 'You must be crazy!' He said, 'That's right, I'm crazy!' And I laughed. I was in the middle of the biggest fight in history at the time and I was being tickled. I hit him and I said, 'You've gotta be crazy.' He said, 'Yeah, I'm crazy, I'm crazy.'

MICHAEL: I often wonder, and I've seen you do this at close quarters to Frazier particularly, I wonder how much you mean what you say about him? I mean you've called Frazier all kinds of awful things – called him a dumb nigger—

ALI: I didn't say that.

MICHAEL: Well you said something like that.

ALI: You said that.

MICHAEL: No, you said something like that.

ALI: You called me a nigger?

MICHAEL: No. What I was saying is that you called him an Uncle Tom, you called Frazier an Uncle Tom. You said he was dumb, you said he was stupid.

ALI: I said he was ignorant.

MICHAEL: Ignorant, all right, ignorant. Same thing.

ALI: He is.

MICHAEL: You called Foreman the Mummy.

ALI: He was.

MICHAEL: And in fact, do you really mean that? Cos I don't think you do, you see.

ALI: Well naturally he wasn't a mummy, but he moves like one. You ever watch horror pictures? Here's a fella now, he's in a spooky castle, he's coming through the woods and here comes the old mummy coming through the woods and he sees the mummy and he breaks out running. And he just can't get away from that mummy! All of a sudden you look up, you've just ran twenty miles at a speed of fifty mile an hour. He's trying to figure out which way he should go and the mummy gets him! I just couldn't see no mummy catching me.

MICHAEL: Do you think you'll retire as world champion?

ALI: I hope to. I can't really say but I hope so. I don't think I'll be beaten in the next five years.

MICHAEL: Next five years? You'll be thirty-seven then.

ALI: Right. Sugar Ray Robinson fought when he was forty-two, Archie Moore fought when he was fifty-one. I'm greater than all of them. Thirty-seven's young. Jersey Joe Walcott won his title at thirty-seven.

MICHAEL: But how much more difficult do you find it to keep in trim, the older you get?

ALI: It's not difficult, it's just hard. Because having money and knowing that you don't have to get up early in the morning, knowing that they're having a party down here and all the foxes and all the pretty ladies are going and they're dancing and knowing you have to go to bed, and you hear the music playing – can't stand it, can't stand it baby! And you wanna get up and go. That's the hard part. You know, when you were hungry and nobody knew you and you were scuffling and then it was kind of easier, I had to do. And now I know I don't have to do. That I have the best cars, Rolls-Royces, I drive them, I don't walk no more. I gain weight quick and my wife is always cooking good food and I live good and I make plenty of money and all kind of offers and it's hard to get up and go. I should be running. I'm twelve pounds heavier now than I was a month ago this time.

MICHAEL: As quickly as that you put that on?

ALI: Yeah, some people gain, some don't. I gain. But this wouldn't have happened ten years ago . . .

MICHAEL: How much do you think you help your people?

ALI: I don't really know . . . Like for an example I would say our religious leader in America, Elijah Muhammad, leader of all the Muslims in America, who is converting our women, cleaning up our people and giving them high morals, teaching them their names, their language, their culture, where they were from before they were made slaves. His teachings are so powerful it has now reached here in London, England . . . He said something that helped two black sisters from near here. They took off their pants, they took off the mini-skirts, they wear the long robes now, the head pieces, they're just like the Muslims in America, and they follow him to his word.

MICHAEL: What's wrong with the mini-skirts, what's wrong with hot pants?

ALI: Well, see, this is a European design thing. You go to Saudi Arabia and tell the women to put on a mini-skirt. Go to Zaire, Africa, have the women put on short dresses. They'd be fined or locked up. Go to Pakistan, or go to – all throughout the black Islamic Muslim countries. Number one, I have a wife and she's walking around with a skirt up to here and then what's happening, why would I want anybody to see her? People look and they're weak and they're lusting for her, all kind of freaks and no-good people on the streets. Horses show their behinds, cows and animals and mules. Human beings don't walk around with their behinds out. Savages walk around with their behinds out. And my wife's behind ain't for every man to look. You understand what I'm saying? Makes a lot of sense. So how can I protect my woman if she's half naked and some sadist run up and grab her? Anything God made precious, nature hides it. You cannot find diamonds easy, you have to dig and dig and dig. You cannot find gold. Everything God made valuable he made hard to get. Ain't a woman more important than some diamonds or some oil or some gold? I won't have my daughter, my wife or my woman walking around for a man . . . What do you mean what's wrong with walking around half naked? That don't look bad to you because you're of the European nature and the black people are righteous, and the Europeans have made them unrighteous.

MICHAEL: But look, I mean before you go on, there are lots of black tribes where nudity is their dress. They walk around naked and there's nothing wrong in that either.

ALI: They don't look at it like you do, and I don't know enough about them. They're savages.

MICHAEL: They're not savages – we were all savages at one point.

ALI: They were savages and we don't style after them. We're talking about the ones who went out into the jungles and started living a beast-like life. You don't know all about the history of Africa and how it started and this and that, but there are civilised people there too, and these are the ones we follow. I want to see two people take a bow to show us how our women dress and how my wife dresses.

MICHAEL: Sure, that'd be interesting. Let's look at that.

ALI: [Turning to face the audience] Sisters stand up who've been converted to our movement in America. [Two ladies in full Islamic dress stand up] This is the way our women dress. These are women, right. Do they look bad to you? Ain't that beautiful. That's the way the black woman should look, that's how she should walk around, that's the way our women look . . . There are thousands and thousands and thousands of women in America, in every city you see this take place. You understand, they're clean, they should serve God, Allah, they don't serve some English clothes designer, they serve God, and they're proud of it and what's wrong with that? You ask me what's wrong with a mini-skirt, what's wrong with that?

MICHAEL: There's nothing wrong with that.

ALI: What man wouldn't want his woman covered up? He can go to work knowing that she ain't somewhere flirting, some man chasing down the street for her behind part. What's wrong with that?

MICHAEL: I don't think there's anything wrong with it all, no, not at all.

ALI: That's because you're white and your nature's not righteous.

MICHAEL: Listen, it's not because I'm white and you're black. I mean, that's nonsense and you know it.

ALI: Your nature is not righteous.

MICHAEL: You're making some incredible assumptions about me.

ALI: The truth is you don't mind your woman walking around half nude.

MICHAEL: No, course not.

ALI: Well then, that means you're not righteous.

MICHAEL: Well then let me put a point to you.

ALI: Half nude. And you're a Christian, too?

MICHAEL: I'm a non-believer if it comes to that.

ALI: If you're a non-believer in God then I understand why you don't care about—

MICHAEL: I believe in my own kind of God, like a lot of people do. I believe in some kind of being.

ALI: God created man in his own image, but you made God in your own likeness.

MICHAEL: Well that's, you know, I mean we can all quote clichés like that. But let me put a quote to you from a book written by a friend of yours, Budd Schulberg—

ALI: Hold on, he's an associate, not a friend.

MICHAEL: Well, an associate.

ALI: Not a friend, an associate. I've got to lecture you on friendship. Friend is a big word. He is not a friend, he's an associate. You are an associate. I can't say Michael Parkinson was my friend. That's a lie, you are an associate.

MICHAEL: But a man who has known you for a long time.

ALI: Yeah, right, not for a long time. He's known me for the few minutes he's around me every so often.

MICHAEL: And wrote a very good book about you.

ALI: Who?

MICHAEL: Schulberg did.

ALI: I never read the book.

MICHAEL: You didn't read the book? Well let me tell you it is a very good book indeed. But he points out one or two things that interest me about you. I mean all the contradictions in you that are fascinating, that people forgive you. Now can I just put one to you that he says? He says, 'He's devoted to a religious movement that looks on the white race as devils whose time of deserved destruction is at hand, and yet keeps in almost daily touch with white friends like Gene Kilroy and Al Conrad. In fact, he's got more genuine white friends than almost any black fighter I've ever known.' Now isn't there a contrast there? You belong to a faith which teaches separatism, which we talked before about when you came on my programme. Yet here, and I know it's true, I've seen it, you have white friends.

ALI: You say I've got white friends. I say they're associates.

MICHAEL: You don't have a single white friend?

ALI: No.

MICHAEL: What about someone like Angelo Dundee?

ALI: No, he's an associate. And I don't have one black friend hardly. A friend is one who would not even consider giving his life for you, that's a friend. The one who would not even think about it. A friend is one who has always got a desire to give and keep back nothing. Always a desire to give and not look for nothing in return. Everybody you name are with me for money. And for what they can get. I don't have no friends. I wrote a poem that says:

Friendship is a priceless gift, that cannot be bought
    nor sold,
But its value is far greater than a mountain made of
    gold.
For gold is cold and lifeless, it can neither see nor hear
And in time of trouble it is powerless to cheer.

Gold it has no ears to listen, no heart to understand.
It cannot bring you comfort or reach out a helping
    hand.
So when you ask God for a gift, be thankful if he
    sends
Not diamonds, pearls or riches but the love of real
    true friends.

See friends are very rare. So what I'm trying to say is this – I've got a lot of white associates. Elijah Muhammad, the one who preached that the white man of America, number one, is the devil, he's been preaching, he's never mentioned England. England's people have never lynched us, raped us, castrated us, tarred and feathered us, burned us up, pulled our eyes out, stuck knives in pregnant women's stomachs, enslaved us, robbed us of our name, our knowledge. Elijah Muhammad's been preaching that the white man of America, God told him, is the blue-eyed, blond-haired devil. No good in him, no justice. He's going to be destroyed, his rule is over. He is the devil. Now Elijah Muhammad preaches that, and I follow him and the white people of America know Elijah Muhammad, they tap his telephone, they know we're there, we're a million five hundred thousand, two million five hundred thousand strong, we're all over America and nobody yet attacks us as being liars. No white man says, 'We are not a race of devils. Come to court, Elijah, you are lying.'

Our goal is to separate and have our own country, clean
up ourselves, quit fighting, quit killing one another, quit
disrespecting all men. The Muslims in America, we're the
most respectable, we're the most respected people in
America. We're the cleanest. We're trying to be righteous
and we're tired of begging white people. We want to clean
up ourselves and have our own country, have our own land
and rule ourselves and quit forcing ourselves on people
who don't want us. Now, what's wrong with this? I have
an associate who works in my camp, happens to be white.
White people don't love black people. It's a fact that white
people hate the black people.

MICHAEL: Well it's not true.

ALI: You're the biggest hypocrite in the world if you go on
nationwide TV and tell me white people don't dislike black
people.

MICHAEL: I don't dislike black people.

ALI: Now I'm a hypocrite cos I got a white fellow working
for me in an all-white country? I'm a hypocrite cos I've got
white fans? So why d'you read something like this? You
ain't used to no black man and mainly no boxer having no
sense. I'm not just a boxer, I'm taught by Elijah Muhammad,
I'm educated. Even Oxford University, your biggest seat of
learning, offered me a Professorship in Philosophy and
Poetry to come in and teach. I'm not just an ordinary
fighter, I can talk all week on millions of subjects and you

do not have enough wisdom to corner me on television. You do not have enough – you're too small mentally to tackle me on nothing that I represent. I'm serious. You and this little TV show is nothing to Muhammad Ali. You've got some more questions, then ask them, and I bet you I'll eat you up right here on air. There ain't no way you can tackle me. All of you are tricky. That's how you, John Hawkins, the white Englishman, tricked us out of Africa to America. You get me on your show and ask me all kind of trickery. You're ready for me. Budd Schulberg said, this is a big bomb he's going to drop on me now.

MICHAEL: What are you talking about? What bomb?

ALI: Budd Schulberg says you've got white men working in your camp. I'm supposed to be trapped now and look bad. How're you going to trap me? You're a white man and your knowledge ain't nothing to a Muslim. How're you gonna get on your TV and trap me? Ain't no way. You can't beat me physically, nor mentally. You are really a joke. I'm serious. This is a joke! You can read this damn book all you want and my leader's Elijah Muhammad who preaches the doom of America and the biggest white people in America, who are wiser than you here, they don't tackle us. Now how are you gonna get me on your TV show and get something ready for me? You had to have it all planned. I didn't know you had a book waiting for me and you were gonna ask me all this. Behind stage you're so nice and you're so, 'Oh, we'll have a nice talk,' and then you get me on the TV. This is a serious thing you got me with. You are contradicting – you're attacking my religion. You're turning white people who are associates, making like I'm thinking they're devils and I'm bad, and you got me on a TV show to say this, and this is the death question. Suppose I couldn't answer that and you had me cornered?

MICHAEL: A likely story.

ALI: Yeah, you laugh now because I caught you.

MICHAEL: Must have been a good question I asked you because you've been talking for about fifteen minutes.

ALI: I'll talk for twenty more.

MICHAEL: That's right, I know that.

ALI: That's right.

MICHAEL: Listen, we've got some response from the audience over there now, so let's throw it open, shall we, to some people over there, perhaps we might ask a question of you. There's a guy in the audience in fact up there, Brian Clough. Do you have anything to ask of Muhammad Ali?

BRIAN CLOUGH: Muhammad, nice to see you again. Are you having a nice time in England?

ALI: Yeah, all but now.

BRIAN CLOUGH: Well I'm sorry about that. If it'd of been a fight, of course, in the last quarter of an hour, you blew your top and you would of lost. You lost your cool with Michael and he would of won . . .

ALI: [Looking confused] Who is this guy?

MICHAEL: In fact when you left school, Muhammad, were you semi-literate in the sense that you had difficulty reading?

ALI: No, not that type of literate. I have a wisdom that can make me talk to you or an educated man on any subject and if the audience or the people listen, they say I won . . . I had the type of knowledge that Jesus had, Moses had, Abraham, Elijah Muhammad, men who are illiterate according to your educational standard. Moses was so illiterate he couldn't talk. His brother Aaron talked for him. Jesus was a carpenter, Noah — all of God's prophets were uneducated men. This is why he chooses them, because he don't want nobody to take the credit for his success. He's God, he takes them empty and teaches them. So I've been taught by Elijah Muhammad. I studied life, I studied people, and I'm educated on this, but when it comes to reading and writing, I'm not, I may be illiterate in that. But when it comes to common sense, when it comes to feelings, when it comes to love, compassion for people, then I'm rich . . . I love to come on your show because you ask me good questions and I like, I really like, a man like you. You ask me a question here — that was good. But you didn't write that, it was already in the book. You just brought it out, you found that. See, ain't nobody else wise enough to go find that. See, I like people like you, you make me think, you keep me sharp, because I'm a spokesman for my people.

MICHAEL: Angelo Dundee once said about you that you could have been anything that you wanted to be.

ALI: I don't know, no, not just anything, but I think I could have tried.

MICHAEL: Well it goes back to this thing that you have a remarkable mind and you're very quick, and obviously if at school you'd bothered about learning—

ALI: I was bright.

MICHAEL: Fine. So you could have been a professional man, a lawyer, a poet.

ALI: I believe I could of, but I started boxing at twelve years old.

MICHAEL: Yes but, I'm just—

ALI: And again I loved it so well I forgot all about school.

MICHAEL: But then I'm just putting the point to you. Do you think if it'd been different and if you had studied at school, what might you have been then?

ALI: If I got really educated, I would've had more of a white mind. Your real educated people, it's hard to convert them to taking a stand. Real educated people, it's hard to change their minds to give up wealth. They don't believe in a God, a lot of real educated people. Once they get really educated they don't believe in God. It's the poor people who believe in God and go to church and believe. The real educated man gets so wrapped up with books and education and knowledge and he knows why things happen. He don't

A kaleidoscope of a man.

believe no more in supernatural, he don't believe in no spirits or God and this and that. So if I'd gotten really educated, I'd be just like the type of man Sammy Davis Junior is or Sidney Poitier or somebody like that.

MICHAEL: You don't like them very much?

ALI: No, they're my brothers so we get along good. We argue all the time about women. I get real mad all the time when I see them with other women than their own.

MICHAEL: Really?

ALI: Yeah, me and all of them. Say man, after you get rich, why don't you come to the ghettoes. Why don't you come to see your people, why are you always in the Waldolf Astoria Hotel, The Americana? All these girls are blonde and brunette. Why don't you promote your people?

MICHAEL: D'you want another quote so you can start shouting at me?

ALI: Yeah, lay another trap for me.

MICHAEL: Right, fine. It's not a trap at all. This again points out the essential contradiction in there, and there is a contradiction, right? 'He preaches against materialism but fills his garage with a Rolls-Royce, a new Cadillac, a new Lincoln, a new camper.'

ALI: No – two Rolls-Royces.

MICHAEL: Two Rolls-Royces.

ALI: Now, I'll tell you another thing, now, I wish he was here, the man who wrote it.

MICHAEL: Well you know him.

ALI: I preach against material things, when have I ever preached anything against material things? I don't preach against material things, I teach our people that in our religion heaven is on earth. I say heaven is not up in the sky, I mean heaven is on earth. Hell is not under the ground, hell is on earth. A white man has told you heaven is in the sky and hell is underground and he takes everything in the middle. I'm getting the watch for a reason, I have my Rolls-Royces for a reason, I have the things I buy for a reason . . . Elijah Muhammad used to have a little old house. A real house, trying to be humble, and all the Negro preachers of Christianity would say to their followers how can Elijah Muhammad be from God, he lives in a shack. Shouldn't God be able to bless him with a nice home? He wanted to be humble, he could have had a big home. He drove a little old car in his younger days, trying to be humble. But they think you don't have nothing. People don't respect you when you look like you don't have no money. So I've gotta buy diamonds, I've gotta be the heavyweight champion, I've gotta have a Rolls-Royce, so when I pull off I'm the black man with the Rolls-Royce. Hey my brother, come on down to the Muslim temple today. I want you to hear the sermon of Allah. Well, that's a pretty car. Oh, where did that watch come from? Oh my man, come on over.

And they listen. You've got to have something. Most people will join a church. You get a Catholic church, any kind of a church, and build a church and put gold seats in it, put diamond-carved speakers on the wall, put carpet in that church and watch how many followers you have in your church. Let another man preach a better word of God, let him have a little house with a store front and he won't have no followers. In this world, we love wealth. They respect people with money. So I have to buy these things, line them up. I'm fixing up a home in Chicago. English-style house, fourteen bedrooms, sixty years old and it would cost a million dollars to build and I only paid a hundred thousand for it. I'm putting all new furniture from Beirut, Lebanon. It's gonna be a plush, plush house. I'm never home, but when I invite people over to talk to me and they ding – punch the bell – dong. And a chauffeur comes to the door. Oh yes, Mr Ali will be out in twenty minutes. I have to sit upstairs for thirty minutes and make him wait so he'll appreciate me. I don't run to the door, I don't run right to the door and answer him. You meet the Queen of England, I bet ya, you don't walk right in and meet the Queen. You sit there for a while and they take you to this room, and you sit there. Queen's probably sitting there watching the news. They make you wait. Make you think about what you're gonna do. So I'm trying to convert, I'm trying to wake up my people and help them, so I have to have these things otherwise I'm broke. So everything I do's for a purpose and I'm seriously working for my people – that's all. I don't expect you to feel like I do, I don't feel about your people like you do, isn't nature. And this thing in boxing is serious with me. When you see me in a ring fighting, it's not just to prove I'm gonna beat this man, it's to beat this man and go back to Chicago and walk Skid Row. Go to Harlem where the black people are taking needles every day. Dope is a big thing in America now. People die. Black women are walking the streets prostituting themselves. When Muhammad Ali come out, for one hour they're righteous. So my fighting is for a purpose – to praise Allah, represent Allah, and go back to America and walk the streets of my downtrodden people. I can say it loudly on television here. I'm the only big million-dollar-making black man in a white man's world of prestige who speaks to his people a hundred per cent and don't give a damn about the money. I love my people and I'm not gonna sell them out, make my movies and mislead them and marry blondes, because I'm one Negro who the boss let in the castle. So that's why I fight. So now you know, from now on in, Muhammad Ali signed to fight for the freedom of black people. Now God is involved. Now you're fighting a spiritual holy war when you face me now.

MICHAEL: When you're fighting Joe Frazier, is that a spiritual holy war?

ALI: Yes, sir!

MICHAEL: Why?

ALI: Cos he's the Uncle Tom.

MICHAEL: Oh he's not an Uncle Tom.

ALI: He insists on calling me Cassius Clay when even the worst of the white men was recognising Muhammad Ali. He keeps saying Clay, he's still Clay, he's gonna stay Clay and for me he will always be Clay. He represents him. I know more about Joe Frazier than you do.

MICHAEL: Well he came from a very, very humble background.

ALI: I don't care, he's the other type of Negro. He's not like me. There are two types of slave. Joe Frazier's worse than you to me. Joe Frazier is a brother but he's the enemy. He represents everything and stands for everything. Two black women in Salt Lake City, Utah – we boxed exhibition before I came over here and the black women had on tight G-strings and mini-skirts and they were going to escort us into the ring. And I said to the manager of these ladies – you want me to walk out there with my women half naked before all of these men with all kind of nasty thoughts on their minds. I said, I won't do exhibition night, I'm walking out. I'm not going to be guilty for parading them before people. I said the damn exhibition's off. Joe Frazier says, 'The hell, the hell is up with you man? Come on baby,' and he went on out with these women. So I'll beat his behind for that! I wanna get him for that! That's what I mean when I say Uncle Tom. See, he's a brother. One day he might be like me, but as now he works for the enemy . . .

MICHAEL: I enjoyed being on your show.

ALI: I'm glad I came.

Chapter 7

THE ROAD TO THE FOURTH PARKINSON INTERVIEW

1974–1981

With President Gerald Ford. Completing the journey back into the hearts of all Americans.

Chapter 7

'It ain't gonna be easy. He's good and I'm good, and that's what fights should be about.'

Joe Frazier

LI basked in the glory of being the heavyweight champion of the world. He was back doing what he was born to do. Fame fed him, he craved the limelight and, unlike many with his level of fame, he didn't lock himself away or surround himself with security guards, but took pains to be close to his public, never declining an autograph request, a handshake or a kiss. In return the general public and the press received him with open arms. He was named *The Ring*'s 'Fighter of the Year', 'Sportsman of the Year' by *Sports Illustrated*, and invited to the White House by President Ford.

It had been some journey back into the hearts of the American public. Eight years before, after he had won the world heavyweight championship for the first time, the same *Ring* magazine refused to designate a 'Fighter of the

Year', declaring that 'Cassius Clay most emphatically is not to be held up as an example to the youngsters of the United States'. But times they were a-changing and the USA was a very different place; youngsters held very different views.

Post-Watergate and the continued horror of the Vietnam War had turned Ali into a beacon of hope, a paragon of virtue with his victories against all odds, his flights of fancy and his sense of theatre offering a welcome relief from the world inside and outside America. He was the anti-authoritarian, anti-war generation's pin-up boy.

Ali, on the other hand, had not mellowed one jot. He continued to stress his omnipotence as a fighter, to spew invective about his rivals, in particular Joe Frazier, and still steadfastly espoused the credo of his mentor Elijah Muhammad. The difference was now he was spouting off in more enlightened and liberal times, and it jarred even more than when he had first begun to proclaim.

And then on 25 February 1975, Elijah Muhammad died. The Nation of Islam changed, and with them so did Ali. There had always been more than a hint that Ali's public pronouncements and personal feelings were at war. He was always uncomfortable with the notion that all white men were evil, particularly given the fact that the most important positions in his camp were held by white people. After Elijah came his son Wallace, who refined the dogma of the Nation, peeled away the more eccentric aspects of Elijah's interpretation of Islam, and began to teach the message that colour didn't matter and that it was no good blaming the problems of the black man on other people. Now Ali could speak openly. 'I don't hate whites. That was history . . . We Muslims hate injustice and evil, but we don't have time to hate people. White people wouldn't be here if God didn't mean them to be.'

I don't believe that Ali ever truly totally bought into the creed of Elijah Muhammad. What he bought into was the need for a philosophy to show black people that they were at least equal if not better than the whites, and therefore encourage them to aim higher than previously. It also gave an outlet to his feelings of resentment and anger at what he had seen and experienced as a young man. But as with us all, time had mellowed him, and it is interesting to wonder whether his violent reaction to the question I posed in 1974 about the number of white friends he had, whilst partly caused by his deep unease about his reading ability, was also driven by the increasingly conflicted thoughts of the inner and outer Ali.

And then came the fight – the 'Thrilla in Manila', on 1 October 1975 – that defined him as a warrior and diminished him as a man. The fight took place in almost unbearable heat. It was fourteen rounds of the most brutal, terrifying, sustained assault by both men on each other. Frazier wasn't capable of coming out for the fifteenth and it is doubtful if Ali could have continued. Such was his dehydration that he passed out in his corner. Pacheco called it 'the toughest fight I've seen in my life'. Ali said 'it was the closest thing to dying'.

For both men this fight diminished them as fighters, drawing the sting from them, with only Ali deciding it

King Ali and his court. Left to right: High Chamberlain Dundee and his assistant Wali Muhammad, Ali, Physician Pacheco and the Court Jester Bundini Brown.

was a good idea to fight on. But it had exorcised some of Ali's hatred for Frazier, as if the bile had oozed from his body via his boxing gloves. Whilst they would never be close, both looked at each other with a new-found respect.

Ali was now the most popular and famous man in the world, loved by white and black alike, but his private life was beginning to unravel. Things were not all sweetness and light in the Camelot of King Ali. His entourage had swollen to such a size that in Manila he needed more than fifty rooms.

The entourage was now no longer dominated by solemn, clean-living Muslims, but by streetwise hustlers keen to make a quick buck out of Ali's name. Perhaps the busiest member of the camp was Lloyd Wells, who procured women for Ali. Ali had always had an eye for the ladies, but now his affairs were an open secret, in direct conflict with his publicly stated Islamic beliefs on fidelity. His second marriage collapsed on the eve of the fight when his wife Belinda learned about the presence of his latest mistress in Manila.

For many close to him the solution would be to leave the stage. The aftermath of the Thrilla in Manila seemed the perfect time to retire, with his fame and reputation at its zenith. But Ali was like a child born in a circus trunk.

Boxing was in his blood. He was defined by his acts in the ring and he craved the limelight and adulation.

So the world held its breath as Ali saddled up his faithful mount and went in search of adventure. But this was not the Ali who with messianic zeal had chased down the holder of his stolen belt. This was Ali as ringmaster, taking his huge circus on tour, replete with clowns, charlatans, tricksters and medicine men, and pitching his big top in towns and countries far and wide. Watching Ali in these years became a bit like seeing Frank Sinatra on his umpteenth farewell tour. The enjoyment was in the reminiscence of past greatness. Like the voice of the century, 'the greatest' was over the hill. The difference was that the worse Ol' Blue Eyes would have to endure was a bum note. For Ali, despite picking plenty of bums to fight, the risk was he could get seriously hurt, which he did when fighting Ken Norton for the third time, and the hard-hitting Earnie Shavers.

It was after the Shavers fight that the first inkling of the damage Ali was doing to himself became evident. Ferdie Pacheco was sent a report after the fight showing that Ali's kidneys were not filtering blood and turning it into urine but filtering pure blood. His health was disintegrating. Pacheco sat down and wrote a letter to Ali, attaching a copy of the medical report, and also sent copies to Herbert Muhammad, Ali's third wife Veronica, and to Angelo Dundee, urging them all to convince Ali to stop boxing. He received no replies, so Pacheco packed up his trunk and left the circus. He was replaced by Herbert Muhammad's personal physician Charles Williams, who went on to exacerbate Ali's health problems by concluding that his deteriorating health was not caused by being used as a punchbag but because of an overactive thyroid and difficulties in regulating his blood sugar levels.

The physician had been replaced with a witch doctor.

There were too many people around Ali having too good a time with his money for anyone to rock the boat by pointing out that he was putting his life in grave danger. One can understand the petty hustlers who were scamming and robbing Ali of so much of his wealth because they knew no different. The result of their grafting meant the need for cash in this period became so extreme that Ali had to undertake exhibition bouts in the Far East and even fight a professional wrestler called Antonio Inoki for the 'martial arts championship of the world' in Tokyo. However, what is almost impossible to understand and hard to stomach is why the three people closest to Ali, two of whom had been ringside to see the destruction wrought upon him, didn't see fit to even reply to a letter confirming that Ali's kidneys were failing.

But continue he did, for two more fights, when an out-of-shape Ali lost his title to Leon Spinks and then regained it for a third time in a farcical rematch with a bloated Spinks, who had spent the previous six months partying. After a golden period of Ali, Frazier, Foreman and Norton, heavyweight boxing was on the slide, with the likes of Don King replacing Don Corleone as the kingmaker. In the aftermath of the Spinks fight, Ali finally announced he had 'retired'.

Ali had made over $40 million from his fighting career, but a combination of his reckless generosity, trusting nature, and the corrupt and venal actions of much of his entourage had meant that by the time of his retirement, much of it had been spent. As his manager, Herbert Muhammad is an obvious candidate for much of the blame, but many people who were around at the time vouch for the fact that Herbert always did his best for Ali, that he made the best deals he could and there was never any proof that he stole off him. The problem, as I see it, was that Ali surrounded himself with lickspittles. Ali was, as I discovered, not a man who had much truck with anyone who tried to defy or countermand his orders or viewpoints. You either accepted 'The World According to Ali', or you left. One story, told by Norman Mailer in his book *The Fight*, neatly demonstrates this. In a dressing room before the Foreman fight, Bundini Brown, the Fool to Ali's Lear, offered Ali a robe that he'd bought for him to wear. Ali rejected it and chose one that he had been given. As Ali admired himself in the mirror, he asked Brown to look at him and admit that his robe was better, but Brown refused to look at him. After asking him several times to look at him, Ali slapped Brown across the face with his open hand and shouted, 'Don't ever do that to me again.' Not that moral cowardice in the face of Ali's uncontrolled ego is much of an excuse. The actions of people like Herbert Muhammad and Dundee contributed as much to Ali's desire to keep fighting as the corrupt hustlers who ripped him off.

Ali tried to reinvent himself as a 'Black Kissinger', even undertaking diplomatic missions on behalf of the US government to India and Africa. But they were for the most part embarrassing PR disasters that exposed Ali's lack of intellectual sophistication and grasp of wider issues outside the circle of his own ego and belief system. He was adrift, a preacher without a pulpit, a warrior without a war – and then the offer came of $8 million from Don

King to fight his ex-sparring partner and now world champion, Larry Holmes.

It would be easy to conclude that this offer was accepted because of financial difficulties, but the fact is that his finances were well on the way to being repaired by a group of businessmen, including Mark McCormack at IMG, who clubbed together to put Ali's finances in order and make the most of his reputation and fame. He didn't need the $8 million. It was estimated by the people involved that – even if he hadn't fought Holmes and Berbick – he would still have been making over $2 million a year for the rest of his life.

The role of Ali in this misguided attempt to recapture past glories cannot be underestimated. He couldn't live without boxing, without the limelight. He had no way of existing except inside the ropes, and he loved the money. Dundee said: 'Muhammad fought because he wanted to . . . Muhammad was never happy outside the ring. He loved boxing. The gym, the competition. It was in his blood, and win or lose, he loved it to the end.' Pacheco is more damning. 'Ali was like a vain actress who's forty and wants to look twenty again.'

However, in order to fight, Ali needed to be granted a licence, and this is where the story takes a dark and tragic turn. He was assessed at the Mayo Clinic and it was discovered that he didn't quite hop with the agility that he should and there was a slight degree of missing the target on the finger-to-nose testing. On top of this it was noted that there was some difficulty with his speech and memory. Despite this the Nevada State Athletic Commission granted Ali permission to fight. The people who surrounded Ali said nothing, sacrificing Ali on the altar of greed, self-interest and moral cowardice.

The fight, on 2 October 1980 at Caesar's Palace, Las

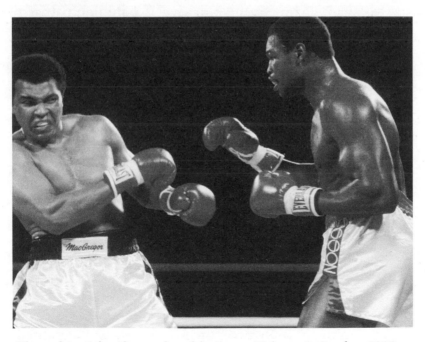

The end is nigh. Ali out-classed by Larry Holmes, 2 October 1980.

Vegas, was a slaughter, Ali outclassed, embarrassed and battered for ten rounds. The end was nigh and the biggest fight of his life was about to begin. The early signs of the battle becoming evident in a London studio a few months before he would fight once more in a baseball field in Bermuda against a man not good enough to wash his shorts, Trevor Berbick.

A fight that on the night – 11 December 1981 – nearly didn't happen because they couldn't find the keys to open the front gate. A fight where fighters on the undercard had to share gloves because there was only one pair, and the end of the round bell was a cowbell borrowed from a local farmer. It was an ignominious end. He lost to Trevor Berbick, punished by a fighter whose presence in the same ring as Ali was in itself the most pertinent indication of the great boxer's decline. The man who had trapped a bear, Thrilled in Manila, Rumbled in the Jungle, had ended his days as a bloated, has-been booth fighter. There are many around Ali who should hang their heads in shame.

Chapter 8

ROUND 4, FINAL ROUND, PARKINSON, BBC TV CENTRE, LONDON

17 January 1981

Our final meeting, 17 January 1981. A bittersweet occasion.

Chapter 8

'If God sat down to create the perfect body for a fighter, anatomically and physiologically, he'd have created Ali.'

Ferdie Pacheco

Before this sad and ignominious end of Ali's boxing career, I did, in fact, meet Ali once more. He came to London to promote a movie, and we thought it might be a good idea to have him on the show with Freddie Starr, who at the time was more famous as an entertainer than someone who 'ate a hamster'.

In the years since our Mayfair encounter, Ali had won and lost the world title. There were worrying reports about his health. Two months after the beating from Holmes, Ali sat down opposite me at the BBC Studios for what was to prove the final, and my favourite, encounter.

First impressions were not good. He didn't shuffle on to the set, but he was slower and bulkier. The features were bloated, the physique thickened, the voice jaded and slightly slurred.

'I'm tired, man,' he said, as he sat down, as if to explain what might follow.

What did ensue was mellow in comparison to our other encounters. The interview had an autumnal quality, a sense that we were both older and more reflective. The fact was we were both on our way out. I was leaving the BBC and moving on, and Ali, for all his talk about continuing his career, was face to face for the first time with his own mortality. He wouldn't, of course, contemplate retiring. He was talking about the rematch with Holmes.

I asked if he wasn't concerned about Ferdie Pacheco's view that he could end up with brain damage. Pacheco had told him, 'You are going to be a shambling wreck. Go to the gym and see these guys that talk funny, that's going to be you.'

Ali said, 'If I had a low IQ I'd enjoy this interview.' He went on to argue that the very nature of his profession meant he was a risk-taker. 'Look at my face. Twenty-seven years of fighting and not a mark,' he said, ignoring the fact that what we couldn't see and were concerned about was the damage done behind the mask.

We talked about alternative careers. He had just made a feature film, so what about acting?

'I've been acting ever since we first met,' he said.

He was on the show to promote a film called *Freedom Road*. In it Ali played a slave who went on to become a politician. It wasn't very good. On the other hand, its premiere in London was the most memorable I have ever attended. Ali was seated in the front row of the balcony, surrounded by his black Muslim entourage, and in the row behind sat his special guests, including Daley Thompson and Freddie Starr. Ali kept up a running commentary during the movie, nudging his neighbours or turning to tell us, 'Watch this scene now, man. This is great.'

Towards the end of the film, with a white-haired Ali on his death bed, he turned to us and said, 'This is a real sad scene. So watch carefully.'

Thus instructed, we watched Ali die a death more melo-dramatic than poignant, and as we did so the breathless silence was broken by a loud fart, which seemed to come from the right of the balcony, then another, which came from the left, and another from directly behind the great man, where sat Freddie Starr. A gifted impressionist, one of Mr Starr's unspoken talents was to make the sound of a person breaking wind and to throw it across a room, thereby avoiding detection. His efforts on this occasion caused consternation on the front row, with Ali's entourage scanning the balcony for the perpetrator of such a dastardly outrage.

Starr's appearance on the show with Ali was a calculated risk, but we just about got away with it, mainly because Ali was the only man in the world whom Starr would concede was more interesting than himself. On the show, Freddie started as he meant to go on. 'All my family were boxers except my father,' he said, as he sat down. I fell for it. 'What's he?' I asked. 'A cocker spaniel,' he said.

During a section imitating singers, at which he is brilliant, Freddie pulled a black stocking over his face, donned dark glasses and did a Ray Charles impression. I was horrified. There were stirrings among Ali's entourage in the audience. Ali looked at me, smiled and shook his head.

If he was angry he didn't show it, but he certainly had his revenge later on when, during a break, with Freddie dancing round the studio saying he was faster and prettier than Ali and was going to whup him, Ali stood and whispered to me, 'Get behind me and grab my arms.' I did so

Ali and comedian Freddie Starr – an unlikely friendship.

and he pretended to struggle free as Freddie – who, by now, had convinced himself he was a real contender – was shadow-boxing in Ali's face. Ali said to me, 'Let go,' and, as I did, he glided forward and flashed five left jabs around Freddie's head, each missing him by centimetres. Any punch, had it connected, would have caused serious damage to Mr Starr's smile. Freddie calmed down after that.

Ali adopted Freddie as his new best friend. At one point, at the party after the premiere of the film, Ali was to be seen working the room with Freddie tucked under his arm like a trophy.

Liam Neeson, the actor, told me of being in the line-up to meet Ali and, as the great man approached, thinking of what he might say to him, how he might distil into a few words his true admiration. When Ali finally appeared in front of him and shook his hand, all he could blurt out was, 'Pleased to meet you. I think I love you.'

Edited transcript of interview

MICHAEL: Good to see you looking really great.

ALI: I'm glad to be here.

MICHAEL: You are?

ALI: I'm getting old now.

MICHAEL: Do you feel old?

ALI: Yeah, I feel like I'm about seventy-three – your age.

MICHAEL: Do you?

ALI: No, I feel pretty good.

MICHAEL: I tell you why I said it's good to see you looking good, because, as you know, there's been a lot of speculation about your condition after the Holmes fight, particularly in this country. There was a suggestion, for instance, that there was brain damage.

ALI: Well I'll tell you what, your brain controls what comes out of your mouth. I'm doing this interview and you check me out and, after, you tell me if I've brain damage.

MICHAEL: I'll let you know at the end of the interview, shall I?

ALI: I went to a place called Mayo Clinic. It's the world's best clinic. There were reports about me having brain trouble, kidney trouble and speech defects, so I went to the Mayo Clinic and got a physical. Stayed there for about two days and was one hundred per cent checked out.

MICHAEL: But I suppose the question people ask themselves about you, and I think it's out of the love they have for you, is they don't want you to go on getting hurt in the ring.

ALI: I never get hurt, it's strange.

MICHAEL: Oh, you must have got hurt in the ring?

ALI: When?

MICHAEL: Well, I saw you fight Joe Frazier.

ALI: I didn't get hurt.

MICHAEL: You didn't?

ALI: No.

MICHAEL: You're a very good actor.

ALI: Are you calling me a liar?

MICHAEL: No, no!

ALI: I've been hit a couple of times but I've never been knocked out. I've never been stopped like Joe Frazier and George Foreman and Ken Norton and Leon Spinks, Earnie Shavers. I mean out to the count of twenty-five, if they counted that long . . . I ain't ever been hurt. Had a broken jaw once but otherwise I've never been beat – even in the Holmes fight, I was just beat up bad. They stopped the fight because I wasn't looking good and it wasn't feeling right.

MICHAEL: I mean, are you serious about wanting to fight Holmes again?

ALI: I shall return.

MICHAEL: You shall return.

ALI: First I wanna prove that I'm qualified . . . Holmes has said that if I can prove myself qualified and I still can fight – I looked so bad that night, until it looked like I couldn't fight no more. I couldn't move, I didn't hit him, I wasn't perspiring, I was dehydrated. Eleven rounds in a hundred and ten degrees heat and no sweat came out of my body.

MICHAEL: But would it be different next time, Muhammad?

ALI: We shall see. That's why I want to go back. And let's say I don't do right the next time, I'll just have to admit I'm finished.

MICHAEL: Why do you need to go back again, because you've done everything – more than any other boxer's ever done?

ALI: I want to prove to myself that I can beat Holmes and I can win my title back. For instance, I'm the only man who had a chance to go for it four times. No man has ever won it three times, so why do we go to the moon?

Because it's there. Why are we trying to go to Mars? Because it's there. Columbus wouldn't have discovered America if he didn't take a risk. So he who is not courageous enough to take a risk will accomplish nothing in life. I'm a risk-taker and the four-time championship is there and I'm the man who got that close to it. So it's something I've gotta do.

MICHAEL: But you're taking a risk, you see, with more than just your physical wellbeing. You're taking a risk with the fans, the reputation that you've built up throughout the world and the love that you feel wherever you go. What they don't want to see is you go and be badly beaten again, ever.

ALI: Forget the Holmes fight, I was not badly beaten.

MICHAEL: You looked badly beaten.

ALI: I saw the film, I watched it myself. I didn't take a bad beating. I took a few punches, but not a bad beating. But I know what I'm doing. See, I've been fighting twenty-seven years.

MICHAEL: That's the point as well.

ALI: I know more about boxing than you.

MICHAEL: That's true. That's true. You have been fighting twenty-seven years and I mean you've seen—

ALI: Look at my face, I can't see the camera.

MICHAEL: You're still pretty good.

ALI: Almost as pretty as you!

MICHAEL: But you've been round the fight game, as you say, twenty-seven years and you've seen what can happen to fighters. You've seen the shambling wrecks that go around, you see them at every boxing occasion. And what people are frightened of is they don't want that to happen to you.

ALI: What, to be a shambling wreck?

MICHAEL: That's right.

ALI: I'm a long ways from a shambling wreck.

MICHAEL: Oh, I'm not suggesting you are now, I'm saying that's what they're frightened might happen.

ALI: Let me tell you why they're frightened. Some people can see farther than others. Some people are pressed with limitations. We all live in a long world of limitations and some people can see farther than others. So therefore when people judge what I'm doing with their logic, it can't be done. Their reason says it shouldn't be done. Their knowledge of history says it can't be done. So their reasoning and their knowledge and their logic clashes with my superior belief. Therefore the result is they don't believe. My thinking is so superior and my knowledge is so positive and my logic is so wise until it clashes with the mentality which is down here, and I'm up there. So by me being so high I can see more and see farther than you. And you're looking at me saying, 'Ali, don't do it! Don't do it! Ali, please, stop, you're gonna get hurt!'

MICHAEL: But you know why they say that. It's for the best possible reasons.

ALI: Because they fear and they are wary. It looks dangerous to them, but it's not really that dangerous to me, you know. It's just another day.

MICHAEL: And it's the affection they have for you. They've never felt about another boxer like they've felt about you.

ALI: Oh, that is so nice. Take this interview for an example. Look how we're talking and how I'm handling you. You're a wise man. And boxers can't do this, even boxers who don't take beatings, even young boxers. This is knowledge and wisdom, this is brain. Look how we're talking. It looks like my show.

MICHAEL: I can't be wise, mind – it's the third time I've interviewed you. The third time you've taken the show. You don't need the money though, do you – or do you?

ALI: I always need money . . .

MICHAEL: But what happens to all this money? Do you spend it on yourself?

ALI: The American government takes about sixty per cent of all of it, and then I have children, a wife, mother, father, people I wanna support.

MICHAEL: How many people do you support, in fact?

ALI: About thirty-nine.

MICHAEL: Do you really?

ALI: You believe me, don't you?

MICHAEL: No, no, I believe anything you tell me – I always have done.

ALI: You're smart.

MICHAEL: Yeah.

ALI: Don't point at me.

MICHAEL: Sorry.

ALI: See, we black folks don't like white folks pointing at us.

MICHAEL: But why do you say that? Do you mean that?

ALI: Say what?

MICHAEL: That you black folks don't like—

ALI: Oh, no, I'm joking.

MICHAEL: You're joking! But you're a public figure and you're one of the public figures who—

ALI: Did you say nigger?

MICHAEL: No, I said a public figure!

ALI: I thought you said you're a public nigger!

MICHAEL: Not at all, I'd never say that!

ALI: Phew! Cos I was gonna hit you, man! When you said public figure, I thought you said public nigger. OK.

MICHAEL: No, public figure. You don't hide from your public. You walk around, you talk to people, you meet people. Have you ever thought about being assassinated?

ALI: See. I wrote a poem.

> Better far from all I see
> To die fighting to be free,
> What more fitting end can be?
> Better that I say my sooth,
> Or the lie remain untruth,

While I'm still akin to youth.

Better now that I lay down,

Now the fear of death has gone,

Never mind another dawn.

If I get shot, or something happens to me, it'd have to be because somebody don't like me for what I believe or whatever I think, and I'd die for that.

MICHAEL: You would?

ALI: See, I know the Holy Koran, the Muslim bible. It says not one soul comes to earth without the permission of Allah, the God; not one soul leaves without permission. When you die, it's time. So I don't believe that it's time for me to die in that way. If it is, then I will.

MICHAEL: Do you have a bodyguard?

ALI: No. I've got one bodyguard . . . it's God, Allah. He's my bodyguard, he's your bodyguard. He's the supreme. The wise one. If I can't depend on him – if I get a bodyguard, I'm telling God, 'I don't trust you.' No, Allah is my guard.

Chapter 9

AFTER THE FIGHT

Still coming out fighting.

Chapter 9

‘Do you have any idea what Ali meant to black people? He was the leader of a nation; the leader of black America. As a young black, at times I was ashamed of my color; I was ashamed of my hair. And Ali made me proud. . . Do you know what it did for black Americans to know that the most physically gifted, possibly the most handsome, and one of the most charismatic men in the world was black. Ali helped raise black people in this country out of mental slavery. The entire experience of being black changed for millions of people because of Ali.’

Reggie Jackson, American former
professional baseball player

Two years after fighting Berbick, Ali came under the care of Dr Stanley Fahn at the Columbian-Presbyterian Medical Center. Dr Fahn diagnosed Ali's condition as 'post-traumatic Parkinsonism due to injuries from fighting'.

He went on to explain Ali's condition: 'My assumption is that his physical condition resulted from repeated blows to the head over time . . . Also since Parkinsonism causes, among other things, slowness of movement, one can question whether the beating Muhammad took in his last few fights was because . . . he couldn't move as quickly and thus was more susceptible to being hit.'

Ali is not the first fighter, nor will he be the last, to have his life blighted by his occupation. We can debate until kingdom come who takes the blame but, ultimately, in the case of Muhammad Ali, the real reason he fought for so long was that which made him a great champion: his indomitable courage, unyielding resolve, unquenchable willpower. To expect him to take a careful approach to his life, to work solidly and cautiously towards a pension, is to misunderstand the soul of the prizefighter. You might as well require a racehorse to finish its days pulling an ice-cream cart as a pensionable occupation.

Arguably, the athlete who was boxing's greatest figure is also its biggest tragedy. The lesson for boxing is that if a fighter as great as Ali can suffer brain damage, then no one is safe. But as with all things concerning Ali there's a twist. Even in death Ali is still causing controversy, still has us arguing about him. On the news of Ali's death the eminent neuro-surgeon Peter Hamlyn, the man who saved boxer Michael Watson's life, was quoted in a *Daily*

Telegraph article making the point that we mustn't be too quick to jump to the conclusion that too many blows to the head were the cause of Ali's neurological condition and his demise.

'We know that neurological disorders follow on from repeated head blows that can manifest though Punch Dunk Syndrome, Parkinson's or dementia . . . We see it in jockeys, rugby players, football players, NFL and boxers. But in individual cases, you never know whether a condition is the result of participation in these sports. Some brains are well suited to dealing with impact: it's a genetic thing.'

This belief that bucks the trend of conventional thinking about Ali's condition receives support from Dr Mike Loosemore, the lead medical officer for the British Boxing Team. He has been on record claiming that there is evidence in Ali's family of a genetic pre-disposition to early-onset dementia. 'His uncle and his grandfather also had the illness, so the story may not be as simple as it first seems.'

For the experts the true cause of Ali's death can never be proven beyond doubt. What can be said is that his long and active career, containing 20 title defences over 15 rounds against some of the most destructive heavyweights, were a perfect recipe for Punch Drunk

Syndrome. What can be said without fear of contradiction is that his deteriorating neurological state was evident for all to see even before the Holmes fight and the people around him didn't once try to save him from himself.

We didn't meet again after 1981. In 2000, when Ali was voted Sportsman of the Millennium, he went to collect his award at the BBC TV Centre. A friend who looked after him when he arrived there told me that, as they made slow progress to his dressing room, Ali started talking about the *Parkinson* shows he had done at the centre. He asked if there was any way he could see them during his long wait for his moment in the spotlight. Then he sat and watched a couple of shows making remarks like, 'This is a good bit coming up', and commenting, 'Watch this – it's where I get him.' Meaning he was about to dazzle a bemused host.

As the years went by, I grew to admire and like him more and more, and never more than on that last occasion we met, when I observed him dealing with his diminishing faculties with faultless courage and humour that has, again in Peter Hamlyn's opinion, helped raise worldwide aware-ness of Parkinsonism and transformed the way boxers are looked after in and out of the ring. Despite being cloaked by his condition Ali retained an immensely powerful personality and presence. He was still capable of 'shaking up the world'. On one occasion, the aforementioned Peter Hamlyn, witnessed Ali coming to see the boxer Michael Watson as he lay in a deep coma following his fight with Nigel Benn.

'We had hardly seen any signs of movement until Ali came to stand at the foot of the bed and held out his Parkinsonian fist, prompting what was Michael's first reaction. As a youngster, I had always thought Ali was God, and here was Michael doing a pretty good impression of Jesus Christ.'

I never saw him again but there were constant reminders of the man he had once been.

One such occasion was when I interviewed Will Smith, who played Ali in the film of that name, and affirmed the continuing influence of Ali with each succeeding generation.

PARKINSON, ITV STUDIOS, LONDON, 26 FEBRUARY 2005

Edited transcript of interview

MICHAEL: You've got an Academy Award nomination for portraying a character that I had a couple of run-ins with in my career, and that was Muhammad Ali. It was an extraordinary portrayal; in many ways you must have imagined yourself that it was an impossible job.

WILL: Absolutely. Any aspect of that film is more than enough work for just one movie. It was a year and a half's physical training to learn how to box, and that would have been enough to have to learn for one movie, but then there was the concept of the Sixties in the United States. I'm a child of rap music and the Nineties and essentially we're reaping the benefits of what happened in the Sixties and I really couldn't understand that kind of segregation and that type of blatant racism, so that was difficult to understand, and then the dialect and trying to get the man's voice right. It was just very, very difficult.

MICHAEL: You spent a lot of time with him, of course?

WILL: Yeah, we spent a lot of time together.

MICHAEL: And what kind of relationship did you have with him?

WILL: He personally asked me to do the film, and that was a shock and an honour, and I said to him, 'Why me?' And he said, 'Because you're the only person that's almost as pretty as me.'

MICHAEL: And actually you watched the first showing of the film with him, didn't you?

WILL: Oh yeah, I was sitting next to Ali and his whole family. And so I'm sitting there in the middle of his whole family. And at one point he leans over to his wife while we're watching the wife and he says, 'Girl, why didn't you tell me I was so crazy?' So he was enjoying it and after the film he told me he was honoured and his family was very happy and it was emotional for them. So it was a year and a half of really hard work that paid off.

MICHAEL: One of the things you got there, that not many of us do, was a privileged insight into the world of boxing.

WILL: Absolutely.

MICHAEL: And never mind the man himself, because we've got no idea how fit these guys are, have we?

WILL: Boxers are in the best shape of any athletes. To be able to go ten, twelve, fifteen rounds with someone punching at you. Michael Bentt played Sonny Liston in the movie. And I was having a problem that I was scared, so I was leaning back too much and my trainer was saying, 'Lean in, lean in, you gotta get your spine angle forward.' So just at the time that I decided I was gonna get my spine angle forward was just the same time as Michael decided he was gonna throw a heavy right hand, so I leaned in and I saw it coming. I put my head down and the punch hit me square on the top of my head, but it didn't fly my head back, it compressed my head into my shoulders. I felt an electrical shock and it went down the back of my spine and to both elbows and I had an uncontrollable desire to find my car keys! I'm very certain that I did not want to be punched for a living.

MICHAEL: I did a spar one time with Joe Frazier and had exactly the same thing. . . . There's another dimension too, to Ali, which you mentioned then, and that's the political dimension. And he was, when all is said and done, a very brave man. He took on the government for what he believed to be right. But you must have faced that as well yourself, when you were growing up. You can't have been that removed from it.

WILL: Oh no, I've had experiences with racism and hearing a word from police and dealing with those situations, but being a child of the Nineties, you know, we have a thing called Internal Affairs and it's essentially the police that police the police. So we'd go right to Internal Affairs and report the officer and that wasn't an option in the Sixties. And I talked to Geronimo Ji-Jaga, who was formerly Geronimo Pratt of the Black Panthers. He said what was interesting was that there was a civil war going on in the

United States and that essentially gave the spark in my mind that it was more of a war scenario. Ali viewed the situation with the American government in the same way that he viewed being in the ring. It was a fight – he was being aggressed upon and he had to win or die. And that really gave me an insight into how he was dealing with these situations and approaching the government.

MICHAEL: But, politically, did he make a difference?

WILL: Oh, absolutely. The thing that Ali did, and generally you can always tell about someone's political power by how children of twelve and down are responding and reacting. And Ali was that guy; he was the guy the children wanted to be. They wanted to fight, they wanted to be able to stand up, they wanted to be able to make a difference.

Chapter 10

EPILOGUE

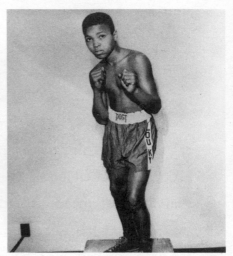

'He who is not courageous enough to take risks will accomplish nothing in life.'
– Muhammad Ali

Chapter 10

ISUPPOSE the aim of this book is an attempt to try and square the circle between the impression of Ali as a man that the four meetings with this force of nature left on me, and the real Ali as revealed in his life story. I can only say with any certainty that my respect and admiration for him has grown immensely, but writing about him is bewildering, and summing him up is an even more complicated matter. How *can* you sum up a man of so many parts, so many moods, so many contradictions?

Thomas Hauser, who has charted Ali's life in painstaking and meticulous detail, believes that the real man is a simple, spiritual and essentially decent man. In the closing chapter of his book, *Muhammad Ali: His Life and Times*, Hauser recalls the time he believes he got closest to the essential

Ali. He was on a night flight with Ali, returning from a trip to Indonesia. Hauser was sitting slightly behind but across the aisle from Ali and able to observe him in an off-guard moment.

'The cabin was dark, and everyone else was asleep – except Muhammad. His overhead light was on, and he was wide awake, reading the Koran. And in that moment, bathed in light, he looked stronger and more at peace with himself than any person I've ever known.'

But he was far from being an angel. In fact he was a deeply flawed, conflicted person. He was in that sense intensely human. His womanising, bigotry, occasional cruelty to opponents and friends were unpleasant aspects of his character, but everything was counterbalanced by his generosity of spirit, his humour and *joie de vivre*. His fatal flaw was that – like all tragic heroes – he suffered from an excess of hubris, which contributed to his downfall; in a sense it explains how he was able to continue to believe that, as his kidneys failed and his brain withered, he could still pull it off one more time. The contribution of Ali to his own downfall should not be underestimated, but it should also be understood, because he was a natural-born warrior. He loved to fight and also what fighting gave to him: the fame, the money, the adulation. It was in his blood, it was his life force, it was what defined him as a man. He was never going to walk away before it was too late.

However, if I step back and look at Ali's life in its totality, one thing strikes me: Ali was a hostage to history. This meant that the arc of his life was determined not wholly by himself but also by the tide of events at the time of his birth which, when allied to his film-star looks, his personality and unmatched boxing skill, meant that he inadvertently became the lightning rod around which the social and racial upheaval of the 1960s and 1970s coalesced and grew. The timing of his birth also meant that whatever he said or did resonated around the world. He was the perfect fit for an era when technological advance in the shape of satellite broadcasting could beam him into every country on the planet. He became, perhaps, the first global superstar, the first international celebrity brand. And as a result, he became a honeypot around which women, hangers-on, charlatans and cult leaders swarmed, cutting him off from himself and reality. I would never cast Ali as a victim, but neither did he have much control over the forces that ranged about him, shaped his life and at times threatened to swamp him.

What cannot be disputed is that he was a remarkable man, and I doubt we will see his like again. A one-off. A man of his time and for his time, with his range of gifts and maddening inconsistencies making us all wish we had met him just once in our lifetime.

But in the end, and to paraphrase Ali again: 'What's a nice white boy like you writing about a man like me?'

Perhaps he's right and I'm certain if he were alive now he would definitely think he was. So, with that in mind, let's – as I had to every time I interviewed him – leave the last word to Muhammad Ali, The Greatest, The King of the World.

'I know where I'm going and I know the truth, and I don't have to be what you want me to be. I'm free to be what I want.'

So there, enough said, rest in peace.

TIME LINE

Date	Opponent	Result	Location
Oct 29 1960	Tunney Hunsaker	W6	Freedom Hall, Louisville, Kentucky, USA
Dec 27 1960	Herb Siler	KO4	Auditorium, Miami Beach, Florida, USA
Jan 17 1961	Tony Esperti	KO3	Auditorium, Miami Beach, Florida, USA
Feb 7 1961	Jim Robinson	KO1	Convention Hall, Miami Beach, Florida, USA
Feb 21 1961	Donnie Fleeman	KO7	Auditorium, Miami Beach, Florida, USA
April 19 1961	LaMar Clark	KO2	Freedom Hall, Louisville, Kentucky, USA
June 26 1961	Duke Sabedong	W10	Convention Centre, Las Vegas, Nevada, USA
July 22 1961	Alonzo Johnson	W10	Freedom Hall, Louisville, Kentucky, USA
Oct 7 1961	Alex Miteff	KO6	Freedom Hall, Louisville, Kentucky, USA
Nov 29 1961	Willi Besmanoff	KO7	Freedom Hall, Louisville, Kentucky, USA
Feb 10 1962	Sonny Banks	KO4	Madison Square Garden, New York City, USA
Feb 28 1962	Don Warner	KO4	Convention Hall, Miami Beach, Florida, USA
April 23 1962	George Logan	KO4	Memorial Sports Arena, Los Angeles, USA
May 19 1962	Billy Daniels	KO7	St Nicholas Arena, New York City, USA
July 20 1962	Alejandro Lavorante	KO5	Memorial Sports Arena, Los Angeles, USA
Nov 15 1962	Archie Moore	KO4	Memorial Sports Arena, Los Angeles, USA
Jan 24 1963	Charlie Powell	KO3	Civic Arena, Pittsburgh, Pennsylvania, USA

Date	Opponent	Result	Location
March 13 1963	Doug Jones	W10	Madison Square Garden, New York City, USA
June 18 1963	Henry Cooper	KO5	Wembley Stadium London, England
Feb 25 1964	Sonny Liston	W6	Convention Hall, Miami Beach, Florida, USA (Won the World Heavyweight title)
May 25 1965	Sonny Liston	KO1	St Dominick's Hall, Lewiston, Maine, USA (Retained the World Heavyweight title)
Nov 22 1965	Floyd Patterson	KO12	Convention Centre, Las Vegas, Nevada, USA (Retained the World Heavyweight title)
March 29 1966	George Chuvalo	W15	Maple Leaf Gardens, Toronto, Canada (Retained the World Heavyweight title)
May 21 1966	Henry Cooper	KO6	Highbury Stadium, London, England (Retained the World Heavyweight title)
Aug 6 1966	Brian London	KO3	Earls Court, London, England (Retained the World Heavyweight title)
Sept 10 1966	Karl Mildenberger	KO12	Waldstadion, Frankfurt, Germany (Retained the World Heavyweight title)
Nov 14 1966	Cleveland Williams	KO3	Astrodome, Houston, Texas, USA (Retained the World Heavyweight title)
Feb 6 1967	Ernie Terrell	W15	Astrodome, Houston, Texas, USA (Retained the World Heavyweight title)

Date	Opponent	Result	Location
March 22 1967	Zora Folley	KO7	Madison Square Garden, New York City, USA (*Retained the World Heavyweight title*)
April 28 1967	Suspended for refusing induction into the US Army		
Oct 26 1970	Jerry Quarry	KO3	Municipal Auditorium, Atlanta, Georgia, USA
Dec 7 1970	Oscar Bonavena	KO15	Madison Square Garden, New York City, USA
March 8 1971	Joe Frazier	L15	Madison Square Garden, New York City, USA (*For the World Heavyweight title*)
July 26 1971	Jimmy Ellis	KO12	Astrodome, Houston, Texas, USA
Nov 17 1971	Buster Mathis	W12	Astrodome, Houston, Texas, USA
Dec 26 1971	Jürgen Blin	KO7	Hallenstadion Arena, Zürich, Switzerland
April 1 1972	Mac Foster	W15	Martial Arts Hall, Tokyo, Japan
May 1 1972	George Chuvalo	W12	Pacific Coliseum, Vancouver, Canada
June 27 1972	Jerry Quarry	KO7	Convention Centre, Las Vegas, Nevada, USA
July 19 1972	Alvin Lewis	KO11	Croke Park, Dublin, Ireland
Sept 20 1972	Floyd Patterson	W7	Madison Square Garden, New York City, USA
Nov 21 1972	Bob Foster	KO8	High Sierra Theatre, Stateline, Nevada, USA
Feb 14 1973	Joe Bugner	W12	Convention Centre, Las Vegas, Nevada, USA

March 31 1973	Ken Norton	L12	Sports Arena, San Diego, California, USA
Sept 10 1973	Ken Norton	W12	Forum, Inglewood, California, USA
Oct 20 1973	Rudi Lubbers	W12	Senyan Stadium, Jakarta, Indonesia
Jan 28 1974	Joe Frazier	W12	Madison Square Garden, New York City, USA
Oct 30 1974	George Foreman	KO8	20th of May Stadium, Kinhasha, Zaire *(Regained World Heavyweight title)*
March 24 1975	Chuck Wepner	KO15	Richfield Coliseum, Cleveland, Ohio, USA *(Retained World Heavyweight title)*
May 16 1975	Ron Lyle	KO11	Convention Centre, Las Vegas, Nevada, USA *(Retained World Heavyweight title)*
June 30 1975	Joe Bugner	W15	Merdeka Stadium, Kuala Lumpur, Malaysia *(Retained World Heavyweight title)*
Oct 1 1975	Joe Frazier	W14	Araneta Coliseum, Quezon City, Philippines
Feb 20 1976	Jean-Pierre Coopman	KO5	Clemente Coliseum, San Juan, Puerto Rico *(Retained World Heavyweight title)*
April 30 1976	Jimmy Young	W15	Capital Centre, Landover, Maryland *(Retained World Heavyweight title)*
May 24 1976	Richard Dunn	KO5	Olymphiahalle, Munich, Germany *(Retained World Heavyweight title)*

Date	Opponent	Result	Location
Sept 28 1976	Ken Norton	W15	Yankee Stadium, New York City USA (Retained World Heavyweight title)
May 16 1977	Alfredo Evangelista	W15	Capital Centre, Landover, Maryland (Retained World Heavyweight title)
Sept 29 1977	Earnie Shavers	W15	Madison Square Garden, New York City, USA (Retained World Heavyweight title)
Feb 15 1978	Leon Spinks	L15	Las Vegas Hilton, Las Vegas, Nevada, USA (Lost the World Heavyweight title)
Sept 15 1978	Leon Spinks	W15	Superdrome, New Orleans, Louisiana, USA (Regained World Heavyweight title)
June 27 1979	Announces his retirement		
Oct 2 1980	Larry Holmes	KO by 11	Caesars Palace, Las Vegas, Nevada, USA (For the World Heavyweight title)
Dec 11 1981	Trevor Berbick	L10	QEII Sports Centre, Nassau, Bahamas

Total fights: 61; wins by knock out: 37; wins by decision: 19; losses by decision: 4; losses by knock out: 1

218

INDEX

Ali, Lonnie (fourth wife, née
    Yolanda Williams) 24
Ali, Muhammad/Cassius Clay
    affairs/womanising 19, 171,
        210
    as an American myth
        14–15
    and the anti-war movement
        57
    army induction tests 53–4
    background and upbringing
        11, 16–23, 30, 73–4
    birth 16
    birth (slave) name 16–17
    and the black community
        11–12, 14, 16–18, 20–22,
        35, 39, 58, 76–83,
        160–63
    black athletes 86
    black Muslims 39, 44–6,
        49–51, 83–4, 97, 183

and separatism 80–82, 150,
    152
boxing style 9–10, 15, 26,
    31, 59
'rope-a-dope' tactics against
    Foreman 133–4
Bradley on 20
on the Cavett show 103
charisma 10, 12, 211
and civil rights 12, 20–22,
    30, 35, 76, 89
Cooper on 3
at Deer Lake, Pennsylvania
    95–6
diplomatic missions 175
discipline and commitment
    26
early amateur record 26–7
earnings 31, 174, 176, 191
education 11, 23–4, 152,
    153, 156–8

PICTURE ACKNOWLEDGEMENTS

The author and publisher would like to thank the following for permission to reproduce photographs:

Tony Triolo/Sports Illustrated/Getty Images, Central Press/ Hulton Archive/Getty Images, Mirrorpix, AP Photo/John Rooney/PA Images, DPA/PA Images, Rolls Press/ Popperfoto/Getty Images, Neil Leifer/Sports Illustrated/ Getty Images, Eric Schweikardt /Sports Illustrated/Getty Image, AP/Press Association Images, Manny Millan / Sports Illustrated/Getty Images, John Iacono /Sports Illustrated/Getty Images, LUCY NICHOLSON/AFP/ Getty Images, CHRIS STANFORD/AFP/Getty Images, Bettmann/Getty Images, BBC, The Ring Magazine/Getty Images, Bettmann/Getty Images, A. Abbas/Magnum